LISTENING TO EXTRATERRESTRIALS

Also by Lisette Larkins

Talking to Extraterrestrials

Calling on Extraterrestrials

LISTENING TO EXTRATERRESTRIALS

TELEPATHIC COACHING BY ENLIGHTENED BEINGS

LISETTE LARKINS

HAMPTON ROADS
PUBLISHING COMPANY, INC.

Cover design by Majoram Productions
Cover art © 2004 Luckypix/Thinkstock

Hampton Roads Publishing Company, Inc.
1125 Stoney Ridge Road
Charlottesville, VA 22902

434-296-2772
fax: 434-296-5096
e-mail: hrpc@hrpub.com
www.hrpub.com

If you are unable to order this book from your local
bookseller, you may order directly from the publisher.
Call 1-800-766-8009, toll-free.

Library of Congress Cataloging-in-Publication Data

Larkins, Lisette.
  Listening to extraterrestrials : telepathic coaching by enlightened
beings / Lisette Larkins.
     p. cm.
  ISBN 1-57174-398-7 (alk. paper)
  1. Human-alien encounters. I. Title.
  BF2050.L366 2004
  001.942--dc22

                                      2004000738

              10 9 8 7 6 5 4 3 2 1

    Printed on acid-free paper in the United States

Dedication

To Harry Bates, the best friend, father, grandfather, or uncle that anyone could hope for. Your love and support have warmed my heart for decades.

To my dear friends Aimee Anderson and Linda Nicholas who believed in my impossible dream a very long time ago and whose love and friendship have meant the world to me.

To Dutchie A. Kidd, for your encouragement, creative ideas, assistance, humor, and editorial contribution. Thank you for your inspiration in writing and contributing the ideal foreword, prologue, and epilogue to this book.

To Robert S. Friedman, the quiet visionary whose strength, support, editing, and confidence in my mission continues to make it all possible.

Table of Contents

Foreword

Someone famous or someone who is an expert in the field usually writes forewords and introductions. I am neither famous nor a UFO-ologist. I am simply a "normal" person who has always longed for otherworldly contact and who has achieved it using the methods described in this book. This makes me the ideal person to introduce it. You see, this book was written for people like me, for ordinary people who desire contact and want to work to achieve it.

Beginning when I was a young girl, I would stare into the sky, feeling the stars envelope me, longing to "hear" from those I knew were out there watching and listening. I wondered if I were special enough for them to pick me. I imagined a meeting where I could touch their skin, feel their comforting energy surround me. I longed for a mutual understanding, in which I could be known for the person inside of me and know another in the same way. I didn't realize it at the time, but that young girl's imagination and longing helped to open a door to receiving all that I had hoped for.

Thirty years and many hard knocks later, I came to work at Hampton Roads Publishing Company and met co-employee, Lisette Larkins. We both worked in the sales department, with Lisette as sales director. She seemed *normal*, at least as normal as any fiery redhead with a mission. She had just finished her first book, *Talking to Extraterrestrials: Communicating with Enlightened Beings.* I grabbed a copy of the book off her shelf, expecting to discover that my new friend was a little bit peculiar. She was writing about holding conversations with beings from space. Not some kind of bizarre language of beeping or strange words but a language I could understand, a language everyone could understand, a universal language. After reading that first book I felt like I had just begun a journey. I had a lot more questions.

That door I had unlocked as a child was now threatening to swing wide open. The words I read seemed to coincide with some part of my soul and I wanted more. I began having memories of things I had forgotten. I remembered seeing a flying saucer. I was sitting on my couch in my home with my children. We were perched on our knees looking over the back of the couch out the window at the huge round ship hovering over our neighborhood. Did no one else see this? Another time, while traveling, I saw a craft suspended just above the horizon. It sat there in the sky almost motionless while we traveled towards it.

What sparked those memories? Had reading *Talking to Extraterrestrials: Communicating with Enlightened Beings* begun this process of remembering? Had the words uncovered a path in my soul? Yes, and I wanted more. I wanted contact, not spotting a ship in the sky but face-to-face contact. If Lisette could talk to extraterrestrials, so could I.

I started reading her second book, *Calling on Extraterrestrials: 11 Steps to Inviting Your Own UFO Encounters.* I devoured it chapter by chapter before it was even printed. I began to embrace the ideas Lisette put forth. The 11 steps she suggests help to mold understanding of contact phenomena. It isn't about being special enough to be chosen; it's about choosing. It is about recognizing the extraterrestrials as the family members they are and embracing them. It is about overcoming pain or fear and moving on, about understanding that the ETs have evolved beyond this world of pain and suffering and are waiting for us to call them forth. These ideas were easy for me to grasp. They felt comforting. I practiced "calling" to the extraterrestrials almost daily. I'm here! I'm ready to communicate!

I began to dream of the ETs often but would forget what had happened when I woke. I would be thinking about them and would catch a glimpse of a thought but lose it before I could internalize it. I felt like someone trying to talk with no mouth, someone trying to listen with no ears. This, however, was about to change. I had learned that you *can* talk to extraterrestrials; I had learned how to call them. Now I was about to learn how to listen to them.

Listening to Extraterrestrials: Telepathic Coaching by Enlightened Beings is the third piece to this amazing puzzle. It teaches how to "hear" what the ETs "say." It gently directs you through a process of relaxation and meditation. It guides you to slow down, open your awareness, and learn to "see" and "hear" thoughts in your heart and soul. This method is a simple, age-old technique and takes only practice to master.

The first time I sat down in a quiet place to try to communicate with the ETs using the techniques put forth in this book, I didn't know exactly what to expect. The words, page by page, resonated with my soul, but would putting it into practice be a skill I possessed? Self-doubt gripped me. However, learning to communicate this way isn't like learning calculus. It's like remembering the taste of a mug of rich hot chocolate after a walk in the snow. It's like looking across the table at a friend you haven't seen for years: no words, just a knowing smile that reflects the lifetime you've shared.

When I first had real, "measurable" results using the techniques in this book, it was light and amusing. The ETs made jokes that only I would get. They encouraged me with warmth of spirit. There was no judgment or condemnation, only a feeling of belonging, a feeling of welcome. Understanding this whole process seemed like a wonderful ending to my lifetime journey and quest. From a very young age I knew they were there. My life path had finally brought me to the point where we, the ETs and I, could sit and chat. But my grandest discovery of all was that this was in fact not an ending but a beginning.

I made contact with extraterrestrial friends who not only want to *talk* with me and *listen* to me, but who understand me and can guide me on my soul path. They murmur encouraging thoughts when I need them. They listen when I rant about a bad day. They whisper jokes when I'm taking myself too seriously. They give me ideas about how to solve problems at work or with my family. They have in fact become a part of my family. I am still new to this process and am still learning, but I have the best teachers in the universe. They are out there waiting for all of us.

—Dutchie A. Kidd

Preface

Years ago I began to be contacted by extraterrestrials. Although my experiences could have easily been considered to be in the classic abduction category, I discovered that ET contact is often part of a spiritual awakening. UFO literature often describes a harrowing process that involves unsuspecting humans being exploited by uncaring aliens. Many experts in the field of UFO research and other well-meaning but misinformed people tend to view ET contact as inherently victimizing because contact can be frightening, confusing, and life-altering. From my experience of more than 16 years of relating to extraterrestrials who have contacted me, I wrote two books in which I discuss how human/ET contact has been largely misunderstood (*Talking to Extraterrestrials: Communicating with Enlightened Beings*, Hampton Roads Publishing Company, 2002; and *Calling on Extraterrestrials: 11 Steps to Inviting Your Own UFO Encounters*, Hampton Roads Publishing Company, 2003).

UFO phenomena have been examined by experts from every angle, and there is no shortage of theories about what the ETs are up to and why. Even those who've been contacted are often loath to explain why the ETs have "chosen" them, and what the goal or purpose is. Despite the fact that their lives have been turned upside down as a result of contact, they are often no more informed about ETs than the researchers who study them. Both experiencers and researchers alike then thrash about, coming up with one theory after another as to the real nature of UFO phenomena.

Instead of guessing and theorizing, why not learn how to communicate with the extraterrestrials yourself?

Those who have been contacted by extraterrestrials usually have turned to the experts to explain their contact and thank God these experts have been available. But this has left those who are meeting ETs disempowered. When we constantly look to others to give meaning to our extraordinary experiences, we disown our role.

Often our limited understanding and limited spiritual perspective render us clueless, and we end up guessing and then advising others of the nature of the universe. In many ways, we're myopic. We're lost in the forest and can't make out the nature and number of the trees that surround us because we're too close to it. So we need a better perspective. To paraphrase Einstein, we can't solve our dilemma from the same mindset that created it. We've got to step back from the forest and get a broader perspective in order to perceive its size and nature. When we do, all the puzzles that were unsolvable suddenly become solvable.

Those who meet extraterrestrials are a new kind of ambassador. As time passes after their initial contact, they should get more comfortable with that role, not less so, as is so often the case. Those who have not yet met extraterrestrials, but desire to do so, are ambassadors-in-training. For the ones visited and the ones who desire to be, there is a communication that enables a conversation to take place between ETs and us. This communication is by telepathy and happens at the level of the soul, rather than being directed by the intellect. Telepathy allows researchers and those who know ETs to "talk" to ETs.

Am I suggesting that *all* beings in the universe use telepathy as a communication device? No, but a lot of them do, based on my own experiences with extraterrestrial contact over sixteen years. Experience has taught me that many ETs use telepathy and are awaiting our readiness to know them. It is easily learned and is a means of communication that, with practice, can help us finally understand who the ETs are and why they are here. For those who have not yet met ETs, telepathy can serve as an introduction. Then you can be assisted by ETs in the most profound ways.

Telepathy allows us to gain a new perspective in which we cease to rely solely on engaging fellow humans to solve our problems and instead seek mentoring from those who have evolved beyond us. So as humans, we might consider opening the dialogue and addressing our questions, concerns, and problems directly to those who are front and center of UFO phenomena, the practicing members of the universal experience—the extraterrestrials.

Once we get the conversation going, we can be assisted by them in innumerable ways. Doesn't it make sense to find a helper who has grown spiritually and technologically? In connecting to otherworldly life, we not only figure out the unexplained mysteries of UFO phenomena, but can create something wondrous—personally and globally.

To many, the suggestion of chatting with extraterrestrials may sound ridiculous. But why? If millions claim that they've been "abducted" then why not talk to those who are "abducting" them? Would many people find that they haven't been kidnapped at all, but have misunderstood the nature of their contact experiences? If many UFO researchers agree that such beings exist, then why don't they put more of their research effort into finding a way to discuss things with the ETs instead of each other? Even among those who agree that extraterrestrials exist, have you noticed that there is very little emphasis placed on attempting to bridge the communication gap with the ETs? If contactees and UFO researchers agree that the two species are commingling, then why not address the obstacles that block us from communicating directly with each other?

Of course, most everyone interested in solving the alien agenda question would love to be able to have a conversation with the ETs. The problem is that we don't recognize how easy this is. Instead, we put our emphasis on getting the government to tell us what it knows about the ETs, or we spend countless hours of research and investigation in coming up with our best guess about extraterrestrials.

I propose that the solution is so simple that it's readily rejected by almost everyone: Learn to communicate with otherworldly beings and start a conversation with them.

Desiring to connect with and be mentored by extraterrestrials is not as ridiculous as it may sound. Our own government was once searching for them. NASA's Project SETI (Search for Extraterrestrial Intelligence) spent over 150 million dollars in the search for extraterrestrial life. So what has been the result of this effort? Suppose that no "search" is necessary—in the classic way that we have defined it—because otherworldly, physical beings are all around us, yet our spiritual immaturity prevents us from detecting them?

This book invites you to recognize that you have a direct telepathic link to extraterrestrials. When you trust that connection, amazing things happen.

Prologue

Once on a far away planet, a family of extraterrestrials
was having a conversation about their neighbors, the
humans, who lived on Earth.

"Why can't they see me when I visit?" asked
the youngest ET of his mother.

"Humans can only see that which their
minds are capable of comprehending,"
she explained. "They used to know us
well, in another time, and another place,
but they've forgotten us."

"I flew my craft through a human city today.
I went zooming over a whole crowd then
circled a tall building and when I came back
around, no one had even noticed," the little one
sadly explained.

"That's quite common, dear, but keep trying.
Eventually, you'll break through. Things are changing.
You'll see."

"But mother, if the humans can't see me, why
can't they at least hear me when I talk to them?
I send some of them strong
messages all the time."

"Most humans have forgotten how to listen
and to speak this way," the ET's mother
explained. "It's a language from
the old country. They've since closed their

minds to it, and to us. They used to know
how to communicate with us, but they've
forgotten that too."
"Then maybe they can remember?" he said hopefully.
"Yes, some are already remembering."
The next day, the young extraterrestrial
was playing in a field somewhere on Earth.
Traveling great distances is easy for
extraterrestrials and happens in a blink
of an eye. The young ET loved visiting other
neighborhoods in the galaxy.
"It's too bad that my neighbors can't
hear me or see me," the young ET thought, sending
a telepathic message to a woman close by.
"If only humans would take time out
of their busy schedules to learn how to detect us."
As Earth's sun slowly set behind a mountain,
the little ET was talking with the plants, making
patterns in the fields with them,
hoping that somebody would notice.
He was contemplating what his mother had
told him. He imagined
how wonderful it would be to meet a human,
face to face. He imagined communicating
with a human, talking away the hours,
exchanging ideas.
He played the fantasy out in his
imagination because he knew that all experience
begins with imagination. He resolved
to try again to contact one
of them.
He believed that there must
be a way to break through.
Suddenly, he knew how to solve the dilemma.
He would first initiate the
relationship with a conversation . . .

Later that evening, a woman was lying in her
bed contemplating the strange lights she had seen
at sunset streaking over the mountains.
It was like a giant lightning bug
that flew over her head then straight into the sunset.
As she fell asleep, she had a dream that she had
met an extraterrestrial and had spoken to it. Was it a
coincidence? First a sighting, and then a dream of ETs?
The next evening as part of her meditation, the woman
again considered her dream from the evening before.
She sent a silent plea into the unknown.
If you exist, I want to see you.
I want to know you.
"Is someone out there?" she asked aloud. She
could detect no response, but as she fell asleep
a bright light enveloped her.
The next day, in another part of the galaxy, the
young ET was again querying his mother.
"Why can't she remember me?"
the ET asked, disappointed.
"Last night I invited
a human onto my craft. We visited
for awhile and then she went home,
but when she awoke the next
morning, she couldn't remember
that she had met me."
"Humans forget that which is too
traumatic for them to remember, dear.
Don't take it personally. They've been taught to
fear us and so they forget us. They block out memories
of our get-togethers when they happen.
Or worse, if they do remember, many
are frightened by their memories and think
we're hurting them."
"Well that's why I wish they could understand
me better," the young ET responded.

"Then I could explain who I am and why
I'm visiting."
"If you want to talk with humans,
you'll have to teach them how,
particularly if you visit them in
their own homes.
You have to teach them how to
relax, and then 'listen' with
their heart and soul. You'll have
to remind them of the language that
they learned long ago, but have forgotten."
"How do I teach them that?
Where do I begin?"
"Begin at the beginning," the ET's mother
gently instructed.

"Tell her who she really is, and who she used to be.
Use a soft voice so you don't startle her.
Tell that we're awaiting her readiness in
order to speak to her.
If she can't hear you in her own home,
then send your message through
some other human—a messenger—one who can
hear you, and then maybe the woman
you visited will come upon your
message in another way.
In fact, don't stop there. Ask the
messenger to teach more humans
the difference between
hearing and listening so that more
humans will be introduced to us,
and they can learn to communicate
with us themselves.

Then, once they learn this
difference, and know our language,
we can be all be reunited."

Every blade of grass has its angel that bends
over it and whispers, "Grow, grow."

—The Talmud

You Can Reach the
Previously Unreachable

The Story behind the Scenes

Consider that there are as many stars in our galaxy as there are grains of sand on every beach on the planet. Some scientists believe that there are billions of galaxies, and contained within each galaxy are billions of "places" on which other forms of life may exist. If this is true, then it doesn't take much of a leap to consider that there's probably a lot of life out there somewhere, and some of that life includes physical, enlightened, and evolved beings.

Suppose that you could actually communicate with these neighbors, as easily as you talk on the telephone. Suppose that once you are able to connect with them, they will help you to uncover the life that you were meant to live. Did you think that humans are just going to stay on Earth throughout the remaining days of our evolution?

But you won't use your mouth to speak words, nor will they. Instead, you will chat using a universal means of communication known as telepathy.

If You Are Reading This,
You May Be a Metamorph

Once you get the hang of this mysterious yet powerful means of communicating, as a metapmorph you will begin to access the wisdom of the ages that can transform your life. A metamorph is a human initiate who is learning to walk between worlds and communicate with others who live there. A metamorph embraces relationships with other physical beings in the universe and *thrives*, rather than becoming victimized as a result of those extraterrestrial alliances. A metamorph is learning to apply spiritual principles to one's otherworldly relationships and understands that all experiences are called to the soul and by the soul for the purpose of spiritual growth. A metamorph knows that there are more inhabitants in the universe than mere humans, and that as soon as we become comfortable with this idea, we can meet them and relate to them.

When we long to explore our relationships with other physical beings in the universe, we can be introduced to them and be helped by them. These extraterrestrial neighbors are awaiting our readiness as metamorphs to know them. When we can talk to these neighbors, we can know them better. Telepathy serves as a vital introduction because once contact is made in this manner, fear dissolves and we can be readied for more types of encounter experiences, including face-to-face contact. Since fear often blocks us from experiencing universal phenomena, telepathy helps us to get our feet wet. It's a process that we can initiate, control, and allow to occur as we are ready, willing, and able. As we become more comfortable with the idea that we can connect to extraterrestrials telepathically, it will sponsor our species toward becoming actively involved in universal life experiences. During this critical time on our planet, we are learning how to become metamorphs.

Metamorphs Are Evolving Humans Who Will Become the Universal Symbol of Coming into One's Own Spiritual Evolution

Imagine hundreds of years from now, when our children's children read their history books and reflect back on this time when their forefathers became the first of the species to recognize that they were not alone in the universe. Metamorphs will be considered pioneers. We will become a symbol for evolving from spiritual naiveté to spiritual sophistication in which we recognize that we are simultaneously spiritual and physical beings and we can connect to other physical, spiritual beings in the universe. The spiritual component of our "being-ness" sponsors seemingly miraculous universal relationships.

Humans are constantly growing, spiritually. That spiritual growth means that our physical bodies can be assisted in adapting to new energies. When we adapt to new energies, our experiences will then change and expand, too.

When a frog changes from a polliwog, is it simply adapting to a new environment, or is it evolving to another version of itself? Is its transformation biological, or also spiritual? I believe that it's both.

All beings grow in a manner that allows them to break into new territory and meet others who live there. That's why you hear news accounts of northern snakehead fish that walk, Koko the gorilla who has been taught to use sign language, and in 1997, *USA Today* and the *CBS Evening News* with Dan Rather reported the Pheonex Lights in which thousands of Arizona residents witnessed the most dramatic mass UFO sighting in U.S. history. Although not yet reported in mainstream news, thousands of people worldwide claim to have floated aboard spacecraft and met ETs. This is what spiritual growth is all about. Every one of us evolves. That evolution is a natural process. Metamorphs embrace that process instead of being frightened by it.

Reconsider Your
Presumed Boundaries
of Our World

Like a frog, metamorphs can adapt to the habitat of the new frontier. That new frontier is the universe. We can know and relate to those who are part of our greater community. But first we must change our self-perception about the role we play and the nature of our universal mobility. We are no longer limited to experiences and relationships that occur on Earth between humans.

Thousands of people all over the world are reported to have had UFO sightings or encounters with extraterrestrials. Humans are spiritual beings, and as such, are not limited by geography or ethnicity. This shift in perception results in metamorphs' evolution into beings that can have experiences with universal beings, on or off Earth. Rather than believing that, as humans, we're Earthbound, restricted only to physical relationships with each other, metamorphs gain otherworldly mobility as a result of their beliefs and intentions and become sponsored by other evolved physical beings who yearn to help us.

Metamorphs no longer buy into our cultural myth that we're alone in the universe. Metamorphs are actively choosing to develop universal alliances, and those alliances can easily get underway with our becoming proficient in the language of the soul—telepathy.

Metamorphs Are
Desperately Curious about
UFO Phenomena

What is this yearning we metamorphs have that propels us beyond our worldly assumptions and has us craving to meet and know extraterrestrials? We are being called. It's not your imagination or wishful thinking. You're being called for a reason. All you need to do now is to take the next step on your journey so you are able to answer them. You will answer by your willingness to enter a portal.

This book will lead you through a process that will allow a spiritual expansion to take place. When we're more spiritually aware, we can see, hear, feel, and experience more of our universe and the beings who are there.

All in all, it's your burning desire for ET contact that will ensure your success.

Knowing, Listening to,
and Telepathically
Communicating with ETs
Is a Spiritual Process,
So Unless We Can Awaken
Our Spiritual Nature,
We're Numb to Phenomena
and Otherworldly Experiences

Most of us are not awake to the universal heartbeat. That heartbeat is a life force that sponsors all manner of divine helpers including angels, disembodied spirit guides and helpers, and physical extraterrestrials. Such helpers pulse all around us, but we don't detect them. Otherworldly beings regularly approach humans, but we don't notice them because we're spiritually asleep. When we're spiritually asleep, it's as though our spiritual battery is low and our vibration—our "beingness"—is dim. It's a vicious cycle because with a lessening of our vibration comes a further decrease in spiritual awareness. So we have to supplement it. Like taking a daily vitamin, we must supplement our vibration by using practices and techniques that increase our spiritual battery, our life spark. Practicing the ideas and techniques in this book can cause a series of reactions catalyzed by your soul's memory of who you are as a spiritual, universal being. Then, when your life spark is energized and your vibration raised, your spiritual sensitivity is increased and you will experience more of the universal heartbeat.

Many of you are looking for concrete steps or techniques on how to accomplish this. Such suggestions of technique are included here, but they will not be useful tools unless you first place your emphasis on comprehending the ideas that set up and prepare you for the practice sessions. This is what triggers your renewal. The ideas here, if considered, will help bring you to a state of readiness for that renewal to begin. As is often said, when the student is ready the teacher will appear. When you are ready, the techniques of telepathy will facilitate a meeting with extraterrestrials, but not until you're ready. Telepathic contact serves as our daily energy supplement. Then, once you understand deeply what you are undertaking here, practice, practice, practice.

A Portal Can
Take You Away, Literally

This book presents chapters I call *portals*. They contain four separate doorways of opportunity with accompanying techniques. A portal is an entrance. Your constant, direct link to otherworldly life can become miraculously evident to you during this process of reading and practicing these four portals. The ideas and techniques within these portals can come to life for you. They are not passive chapters, but portals of opportunity that await your readiness. A portal is being opened for you by the ETs as you consider the material and begin the practice sessions. Can you sense the portals or the ETs? Are you ready to step through? The portals will help you walk between worlds to connect with extraterrestrials. You are offered a gateway to the universe as you remember how to reconnect to your universal family members.

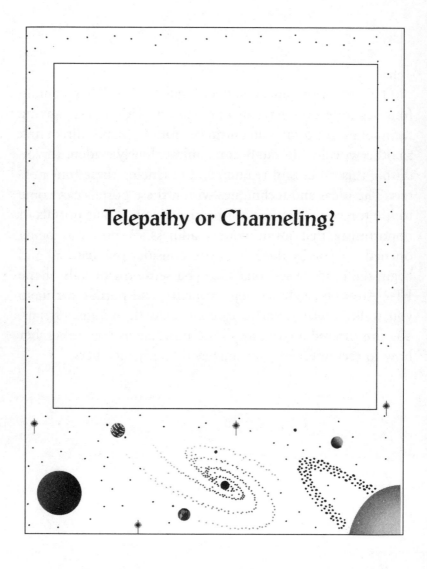

Telepathy or Channeling?

Telepathy is often considered to be the same thing as channeling, although channeling is often understood to be a device linking "sensitives" to disembodied spirits or guides. Telepathy links us to our family members in the universe who are in physical form. Used in this manner, it's a new term considering that we haven't often understood that this linking is possible. Further, in the way that I understand telepathy to occur between ETs and humans, it happens more at the level of the soul, not simply as a mind-to-mind exchange. Telepathy serves as an introduction to extraterrestrial relationships, which can later include physical encounters with beings. Conversely, telepathy can reunite those who've already been contacted by ETs but don't understand the reason for it and who haven't understood that they can have an easy conversation with those who've seemed so elusive.

Ultimately, telepathy can deliver our species to the heartbeat of our physical universe. In the way that I'm using this concept, channeling doesn't fit because the word has so often been associated with an intangible connection with intangible beings.

Unlike classic channeling in which the medium communicates with disembodied spirits, angels, or spirit guides, ET communication occurs with other beings who are very much in physical form and have not yet crossed over. They may actually be located right next to you in the room but are invisible to you. The process may seem like channeling and there are many similarities. But because many people do not recognize that we can easily talk to otherworldly, *physical* beings, I've found it's helpful to discuss the nuances of communicating with ETs using words that more accurately describe the process.

Extraterrestrial encounter phenomena carry so many negative emotional overtones to so many people that I like to give special attention to the manner of communication that is particular to extraterrestrials and humans. I don't attempt to find one word to accurately describe all types of communication such as sign language, verbal language, internet language, telephone conversations, faxing, or video conferencing. They are all forms of communication and they have many similarities. But each communication method is named differently in order to distinguish it from the others. I find that having a special language to explain and describe the process specific to ETs can be helpful.

If you prefer the term channeling, by all means use it. In the past, some people who have written books and communicated with ETs have also referred to their communications as channeling. Many people who have contacted me are having encounters with physical beings, extraterrestrials, and do not always resonate to the experiences shared by mediums or other channelers. I offer material that recognizes the challenges specific to ET contact. As such, I use different words to help metamorphs come to terms with the nuances of their special relationships.

Although ETs can take on temporary, non-physical forms, they are also physical, and are able to shape-shift. My understanding is that there is not one way to describe or label extraterrestrials. Many are enlightened and many aren't. Many are able to appear both in physical or non-physical forms and others may not. To me, the emphasis should be placed upon what and whom you desire to meet and relate to, and then focus on that. I believe that the universe and those who live there include all variations. Spiritual beings are limitless. Decide who you want to know, while simultaneously recognizing that your idea about something can make it so. You will attract that which you expect.

You will be learning to detect extraterrestrials' communication, and when you're ready, to include the sense of sight. The agenda of your soul will determine if you are ready, willing, and able to then see them in physical form. Initially, then, you will become comfortable in listening to the cadence of their telepathic conversation.

Determine Who
You Want to Talk To

Since clear intention is the single most powerful tool of manifestation at our disposal, the metamorph's clear objective in deciding whom he chooses to meet will determine the outcome. There's nothing wrong with connecting through channeling to spirit guides. My approach though, involves interrelating to *physical* extraterrestrials. You will determine who you wish to talk to and know better.

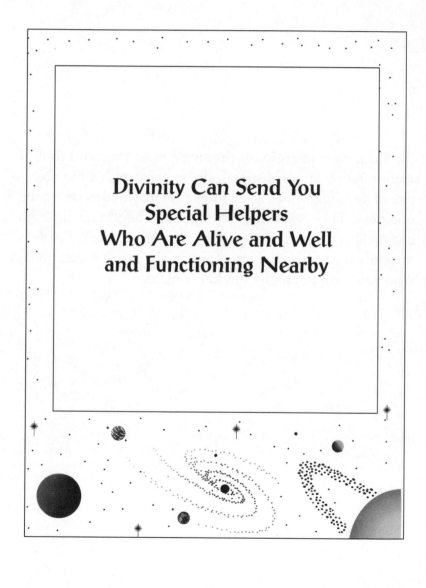

Divinity Can Send You
Special Helpers
Who Are Alive and Well
and Functioning Nearby

These divine helpers are our coaches. They don't have to be disembodied spirits relegated to heaven, the afterlife, or any place else that isn't physically tangible. As easily as we've learned how to use sign language, a telephone, or the Internet, metamorphs are using tools to "dial up" others in the physical universe. Metamorphs connect to extraterrestrials *who exist in physical bodies*. Once we connect telepathically, we can expand our relationship if we choose to.

If this seems too extraordinary, unrealistic, or impossible, that's okay. Most likely this process will be embraced initially only by those of a pioneering spirit; as with all levels of spiritual growth, everybody will get there.

Within the Context of
Universal Law,
Abductions
Are Misunderstood

Given the bad press about the mean old "aliens" who've been doing "abductions," you may be wondering why anyone would want to pursue and establish alliances with extraterrestrials.

People are confused about UFO phenomena because I believe it's been largely misunderstood. In this book, I propose that extraterrestrials have unique qualifications *to help us*, not hurt us.

Whatever you may assume about UFO phenomena, I ask you to leave those assumptions behind and consider it with fresh eyes. Instead of believing that extraterrestrials are exploitive, I'd like you to consider that many of them are God's divine helpers, ready to help us with the next step in our spiritual evolution.

For the most part, classic UFO abduction theory does not consider spiritual law that recognizes that we are responsible for the nature and quality of all of our relationships, whether in this world or another. We can be empowered to create relationships that serve us. When we believe in the illusion that we're powerless to change relationships that we don't like, we're living a lie. That's why it's impossible to enter the abduction debate while immersed in the cultural illusion.

People want to know specifically which aliens I'm referring to because many people have attributed certain characteristics to certain ETs. They want to know if I'm referring to the mean "grays," the friendly Pleiadians, or the victimizing reptilians. I don't make distinctions based solely on physical characteristics any more than I make distinctions about humans based on physical characteristics. On the cover of my first book there's an image of a gray that I describe as "enlightened." I included an image of the gray in relation to the word "enlightened" specifically to make a point because I recognize that UFO literature has long assumed that grays and Pleiadians are not the same type of being nor do they have the same agenda with respect to Earth. I disagree with that entire premise. This doesn't mean that I'm suggesting that every single gray is enlightened, but nor do I suggest that every single gray is an abductor. I understand that each of us will call experiences to ourselves that help our soul to grow. Just because many people describe being victimized by grays, doesn't mean that others don't also describe meeting grays who are enlightened. To me, the process of calling and inviting extraterrestrial alliances means that we've got to get over the habit of characterizing anyone based on the way that they look.

My experiences, and the experiences of many others who have contacted me describe grays who are spiritually enlightened and have dramatically assisted them with their spiritual growth. Even though this flies in the face of much of what is written in the UFO literature is beside the point. I won't adopt erroneous assumptions that negate spiritual law. The fact that this is counter to others' claims who describe victimizing grays is precisely the reason that I've written my books. I'm simply offering another way to look at UFO phenomena. If there are any assumptions made, it's not me who's making them, but the culture as sponsored by Ufology. I more accurately suggest that spiritual law holds true everywhere. You cannot separate spiritual law from experiences on Earth with humans and experiences with extraterrestrials. I suggest that we create and manifest relationships based on who we are, what we believe, what we expect, what we need to experience in order to grow, and our past karma. I have no desire to enter the debate in naming which ET group is evil and which group is good, any more than I choose to label any one ethnic group on Earth as good or evil.

All experience arrives as a result of the goals we give to our soul. Life is a mysterious but spiritual process. There are no random coincidences or accidents.

A so-called abduction, like a bad marriage, does not happen in a vacuum because we are co-creating all that we experience. I'm not suggesting that those who are victimized by others are at fault for their experiences. I'm suggesting that until we recognize that we create our experiences as a result of that which we think about, believe, talk about, and act upon, we will forever believe we're helpless to change anything at all.

It may help to consider that I'm writing about how to befriend others who live not across the street but across the galaxy. From my perspective, it's a naive critic who becomes angry because I won't make distinctions about who may or may not make a good ET friend. I leave those distinctions, generalizations, and prejudices up to you, if you feel the need to make them. My mission is to inspire you to know others who are extraterrestrial in nature. There's a large body of evidence proffered by quantum physics that proves how our ideas or imagination about a thing create its very existence in our reality. I suggest that many beings are much more evolved and enlightened than we are. They exist and are available for friendships. If you're convinced that certain beings who have a certain name or body color are evil then I encourage you to stay with your belief system if it serves you.

Analogously, a dear friend of mine insists that all men are rotten because she just emerged from a nasty divorce and insists that men cannot be trusted. She refuses to have male friends or become romantically involved. If that world view serves her then I suspect she'll keep it for as long as it continues to serve her. But I'm not invested in changing her mind about men. I just offer ideas for consideration. Her prejudices or assumptions are her creation and she may need to go to her grave being offended by men.

So if you're offended by my lack of gossip or warning about one ET group or another, about a group who has blue skin, gray skin, or large eyes, this probably isn't the book for you. I respect your right to choose your world view. Whomever you fear, hate, or are suspicious of is determining who you are. Your opinions say more about you than they do about anyone else. So choose your belief systems carefully because they are creating your next experience.

Prejudices notwithstanding, our seemingly worst experiences often become our greatest teachers. My first marriage was heartbreaking, but without it I would not be the person I am today. The experiences with my first husband propelled me to consider how and why my life experiences were not to my liking. So who is my teacher and who is my enemy? Until we stop pretending that we have nothing to do with the experiences that show up, we will continue to be living a lie. Until we recognize how the soul keeps attracting those experiences that teach us the most, we'll be forever spiritually asleep. For a complete discussion of these ideas, please refer to my first two books, *Talking to Extraterrestrials: Communicating with Enlightened Beings* (Hampton Roads Publishing Company, 2000), and *Calling on Extraterrestrials: 11 Steps to Inviting Your Own UFO Encounters* (Hampton Roads Publishing Company, 2003).

As a result of the response that I received from those books, I decided to write this one. Many people tell me that they long to have contact with extraterrestrials but don't know how to go about it. Often, people erroneously assume that the ETs are doing the choosing. I propose that the manner and quality of our relationships fall within our domain. This includes relationships with extraterrestrials.

Extraterrestrials Are Divine
Strategists Extraordinaire

The role of any good coach is to help the student design a winning strategy in order to thrive. The goal of the telepathic connection to ETs is to be helped by them. Their assistance can come in many different forms. You can tell these enlightened helpers what's in your heart to accomplish in your life and they will strategize for you a winning formula and then coach you in fulfilling it. Everyone has come here to do something. If you don't know why you're here on this planet, the ETs may assist you in getting in touch with your soul's blueprint.

The nature of their help will be determined by your readiness and your soul's agenda. Once assisted by them, spiritually aligned, highly functioning, and thriving humans will most quickly sponsor global healing by their own example. I'm better able to help my neighbor, and help my planet when I'm doing well in every area of my life.

Metamorphs Are the
Spiritual Protégés of ETs

As humans, we are not the guinea pigs of aliens. We're their spiritual protégés. But if you can't talk to these universal strategists, how will you put their mentoring into practice? This is why it's so important to begin practicing telepathy. There's a lot to be "said" between us.

If the idea of having a conversation with an extraterrestrial seems ridiculous to you, I can only nod my head and smile because I remember my own doubt and procrastination when extraterrestrials offered to coach me. I used to be squeamish but I got over it. It took me more than ten years of ET contact before I let go of my assumptions, doubts, and insecurities about this process and became willing to be their protégé. You can too by avoiding the roadblocks that stopped me.

For many metamorphs such as myself, this journey can be challenging, particularly when we are being mentored by coaches who aren't even from our world. The biggest hurdle to overcome is self-doubt. This will be discussed at length throughout the book.

Since many groups of extraterrestrials are highly functioning, spiritual members of the universal community, they have a unique and very broad perspective of things. This is how they help us. Given where we are, in respect to our evolution, we need greater *universal* perspective to grow spiritually and evolve to a more improved version of ourselves. If you desire to meet and know otherworldly beings who are evolved and enlightened, first you have to consider that these relationships are possible. By believing that it's possible, it becomes so. All experience begins with our idea about a thing. This is how you will attract the enlightened ones. You'll believe that you can, and you will.

What Is Your Role
As It Relates to the Universe?
What Are the Goals
You Gave to Your Soul?

Perhaps you have never considered that you hold the key to assisting humanity in knowing its place in the universal experience. I believe this is true for many of us, but first we must help ourselves by embarking on this process. It will be very helpful to humanity to be mentored by our universal neighbors, but the process begins on an individual level. This is why your soul may be calling you to begin. Someone has to get this concept going. How about you? We cannot as a species move to a grander role in the universe until individuals show the rest of humanity how it's done. Metamorphs believe that such roles and relationships are possible.

Establishing a telepathic connection with ETs will help you to believe more deeply in your soul's mission. That's what coaches do. They inspire protégés with hope and hold their hands on the way to a more gratifying life.

Our species' spiritual growth begins with individual spiritual growth. That's why extraterrestrials help us on a one-to-one basis first. One person's awakening can create an amazing opportunity for the whole species. As the individual progresses, so does the group.

Extraterrestrials Cannot Experience Their Oneness without Including Us

You may be wondering why ETs are motivated to help us with that growth.

The answer is so simple that it's often readily rejected. But for those who have even the slightest grasp of spiritual law and how it applies to spiritual growth, you've probably already gleaned that the object of life is to learn how to love. This is what every religion on the planet teaches. Love expressed means putting this message into action. We learn to love and help our neighbor in order to heal ourselves. When we help one another, we help ourselves tenfold. That's the reason behind the biblical teaching that says as you do to another, so shall it be done unto you.

Since humans yearn to grow spiritually, we can imagine our otherworldly neighbors want to grow too, and as such, sponsor humanitarian efforts by helping *us*. They help the group that is desperate for help: humanity on Earth. Almost no one alive on the planet today could argue the fact that the human species is in need of help.

Extraterrestrials understand that for reasons of their own spiritual development, helping us assists them to grow. Enlightened and evolved extraterrestrials comprehend that they cannot experience their oneness unless they establish relationships with their neighbors who are in need of help.

So where will they help us?

The White House Lawn Isn't a Personal Enough Setting for Your First Meeting

If you wanted to meet with somebody important to you, where would you meet? In the shopping mall? Yankee stadium? How about the White House lawn?

You'd probably prefer to set up a quiet, private meeting where there are no distractions. You might not want to practice your new language in a group setting. Within the privacy of your home or some other comfortable setting may be more conducive to your introduction. Many people who have yearned for some type of ET contact have erroneously assumed that they'd begin that contact on a mountaintop by seeing a UFO. Instead, your own home will likely become your launch pad.

Extraterrestrials
Tailor Coaching to
Meet Individual Needs

Enlightened and evolved extraterrestrials are coaching individuals. They contact those who are ready. But first, they're encouraging us to learn telepathy that will enable us to continue with that personal coaching.

Ultimately, the content of that coaching will depend entirely on the type of help that's needed. Do you need help healing from a disease? Perhaps you've been chronically broke your whole life and you desire to experience financial abundance and the freedom it provides. Perhaps you have a scientific background and you have an idea that would benefit all of humanity but you don't know how to proceed. Or maybe you yearn for a soul mate but have no clue how to find him or her.

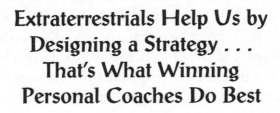

**Extraterrestrials Help Us by
Designing a Strategy . . .
That's What Winning
Personal Coaches Do Best**

Many enlightened extraterrestrials have evolved in an extraordinary way in matters of spirituality, technology, and mastery of their body so they are qualified to consult with us individually to help us strategize our way out of our mess. Those strategies help us map the development of our soul. There is no problem too small, no desire too big, which cannot be strategized through telepathic coaching.

At the very least, those who use telepathy can begin a discussion with the ETs regarding past or present UFO experiences and/or contact. There's no limit as to how one can use telepathy to serve the agenda of the soul. Once our connection is established to extraterrestrials, the sky's the limit and you will be assisted in a way and manner beyond your imagination.

My experiences, and the experiences of thousands of others who have contacted me, with ETs form the basis of my opinions about them. They have helped me to get in touch with the agenda of my soul. As a result, over the past sixteen years I have made better choices regarding romance, finance, and health. My professional life has been completely transformed because I've been assisted in making choices that better serve my soul's blueprint.

When I was contacted by a half-dozen, small-framed, gray, hairless extraterrestrials, I could hardly believe what was happening. Immediately we were communicating, although it took me several minutes before I realized that our mouths were not moving. It has taken me another decade and a half to internalize, integrate, and understand the process of my connection to them. This is why I can help you. I've traveled this road myself. No longer does the process of connecting to extraterrestrials need to be through "trial and *terror.*"

The Flaming Arrows
That Stop Most
Would-Be Metamorphs
Are Fear and Self-Doubt

Today, I'm able to understand and connect daily to the ETs' telepathic communication. The relationship with my extraterrestrial coaches has been extraordinary. But it didn't start out that way. I'd like to help you avoid some pitfalls and so I've identified for you the flaming arrows that will always be pointed at the metamorph who dares to break out of the human mold as we know it. They do not have to prevent your spiritual expansion, but they often do.

These flaming arrows come in the form of:

- self-doubt
- others' fear of what you are attempting
- others' criticism
- our own cautiousness
- fear of the unknown
- belief in the cultural myth that has us believe we're unsafe and disempowered

These flaming arrows are pointed straight at you. Will you succumb to them?

Protect Your Assets

Remember that each of us has an amazing "bank account" of personal assets that can bolster us through whatever challenge or hardship comes our way. Those assets are not financial, but are endowments from the universe as part of our spiritual heritage. The problem is that we don't believe in them. We've lost touch with them. We hardly ever even consider them. Here are some of them:

- We have the right to explore our universe with confidence and to believe that it's not impossible or inherently unsafe.

- We have the right and the ability to know and relate to extraterrestrials without needing our government to act as an intermediary or facilitator to these relationships.

- We have the right to make the world a better place, through our own demonstration of mastery as a result of our universal alliances.

- We have the freedom to be helped to rise above earthly limitations of poverty, worry, and illness.

- We have the courage to dare to dream and to make those dreams a reality.

In becoming a metamorph, you must learn how to protect your assets. Your dream to be deeply connected to your universe is your greatest asset. It can be manifested and modeled to the rest of humanity, if you dare. This asset, more than any other, will change your life experiences, and by modeling it to others, change the world as we know it. We will grow as individuals as we are able to efficiently move onto our higher path and get in touch with why we are here. Once you identify that, you must get started with putting your dream in place. Too many of us lose sight of that dream and settle for mediocrity.

Don't allow anyone to steal your dream from you. Your dream is your soul's blueprint. Humanity's evolution depends on individuals just like you who refuse to give up their soul's blueprint so that the entire species may benefit. You will be assisted in this in immeasurable ways by establishing universal alliances.

**Train Your Brain
to Think Thoughts
It's Never Thought Before.
This Is How We Evolve.**

Over the years, my otherworldly relationships have developed to the degree that I have learned to trust and act upon the content of our telepathic communications in order for me to grow in every manner possible. My ET coaches have addressed all aspects of my "being-ness." They coach me on matters spiritual, financial, professional, physical, interpersonal, and psychological. But I did have to practice letting go of my assumptions in order to reprogram old beliefs. This is one of the hardest things about any radically new undertaking. First we have to let go of the idea that it seems impossible or outrageous.

As I have described in my previous books, it has been an incredible journey. I have learned to receive universal help to walk between worlds by using telepathy as the key to this process.

After getting over the shock of meeting physical ETs and then finding the inner strength and confidence to continue the relationship with them, my life has been transformed in a way and a speed that amazes me.

Extraterrestrials have helped me to think and consider things in a different way. Their involvement in my life has resulted in greater clarity of thought; assistance with my soul's blueprint; personal guidance with issues of health; assistance with my personal relationships; and in my opinion, a degree of coaching and mentoring that meets or surpasses any help presently available on the planet.

To Be Personally Coached, You Do the Choosing, Not the ETs

Contrary to what has been taught in much of the UFO literature, relationships with extraterrestrials are not dictated by the ETs, but by individual humans. The problem is that we don't recognize how our thoughts, words, actions, and beliefs dictate the experiences that we create. We are not randomly choosing the events of our life or the relationships that make up our life. There's order and reason to the seeming chaos called life. When we recognize that we are empowered spiritual beings, we can choose the manner and style of our relationships, whether in this world or another.

We're Merely Remembering the Universal Link That We Already Know, but Have Forgotten

Telepathy is a bona fide communication used throughout the cosmos between universal siblings. It's not a watered-down version of a real language nor is it imagined. It's a legitimate form of communication, just like verbal language or sign language, used for eons by spiritual beings who remember their connection to the universe. Since humans are part of the universal family—although we've forgotten that—it's all part of our evolutionary code to keep in better touch with each other.

Therein lies the key. We're actually not learning anything new at all.

Like riding a bike, we can quickly pick up telepathy again, even if we haven't done it in a very long time. As we've done it before many times throughout the ages of the evolution of our soul, it's time to connect again in this lifetime.

Since many of us have forgotten that we have this ability, I hope to help you rekindle that skill. All that is needed is for you to have a little help getting started. With a little practice, you'll be off and running, chattering and bantering with your otherworldly friends with the ease with which you use your own native language.

By reading and attempting the ideas and techniques discussed within the portals that follow, your soul's memory will be ignited. I hope that this material, and my other books that support it, will help you understand yourself as a spiritual member of our universal community.

Metamorphs Mothball
the Programs of NASA

We need no longer rely on NASA or the government to connect us to our universe. We're growing up and recognizing that we no longer need a parental authority, religion, or government to take us to our next grand universal experience. Metamorphs around the globe have begun their own extraordinary journey with extraterrestrials, so you are not alone in this awakening. I have the letters from readers to prove it.

Telepathy is just one aspect of contact with extraterrestrials, but its use will most easily propel your expansion as a universal being. In addition to practicing it, I encourage you to be alert and notice how telepathic contact may be expanded upon when you are ready. Contact by extraterrestrials is not limited to just one type of communication. Contact comes to us packaged in many different forms and venues. Clues are often left for us, but their meaning becomes our responsibility to discern and unravel.

Those strange and mysterious clues are provided by ETs to demonstrate their existence, and the clues often begin long before we've ever considered talking to extraterrestrials. As you read this, you may already be jolted with long-forgotten memories surfacing in your consciousness.

Soon, you'll become convinced that ETs have taken you on to coach you to strategize through and master your challenges, issues, and soul mission. There is no one alive who cannot benefit from divine strategies such as those.

Coaching As a
Method of Learning
Is Incredibly Effective

In my opinion, personal coaching as a method of learning is the single most successfully used method of learning available. When the coach oversees the protégé's progress to ensure the skill has been mastered, and the strategy successfully implemented, the student masters the course in the fastest, most efficient way possible.

Each of us has come to Earth to do something. Perhaps you already know what that is for you. Or maybe you have no clue but want to get in touch with it. Either way, do you wish to get underway? Do you yearn to play a bigger role? Are you stalled on the road to mastery? It serves the soul to get on with its responsibilities as soon as possible. Too many of us have been delaying our own mastery. Getting in touch with the heartbeat of the universe will help you get going again because when we receive evidence of divinity we're inspired to action.

If you think this sounds intriguing, it is! Venturing into the new frontier of the universe is the greatest adventure of all time, but it all begins with an introduction. Establishing your telepathic connection serves as this vital introduction. So let yourself go, and allow the portals of this process to carry you safely into the universal stream where you will establish your beloved connection to extraterrestrials—and all of the universe.

At this point you may have a lot of questions. Keep reading. Many of them will be addressed in the pages that follow.

There Are Two Pivotal Tools
in Telepathic Coaching:
The Chat Room and
The Pep Talk.
A Lasting, Explosively
Powerful Spiritual Connection
to Telepathic Extraterrestrial
Coaching Requires the
Consistent Use of Both.

First Portal:

The Chat Room

In order to retrieve your connection to your universal family members, you need to find them. In the hustle and bustle of our crazy workaday world, you must set up a special room or area in your home or office that facilitates your connection. In the beginning, you will need to practice recognizing the extraterrestrial voice. In order to do so, initially you must place yourself in a quiet, comfortable location through all the weeks of this training and, I hope, much longer. Later, your chat room can be anywhere, because by then you will have grown to recognize that your chat room stands for taking time out of your daily activities to disconnect from the worldly noise and reconnect with your extraterrestrial neighbors.

Your chat room is a safe, private, quiet place that facilitates your first introduction to your coach. There, you will tell your coach all of your worries, problems, and concerns about anything and everything. Your chat room can also be a special place outdoors under the trees, near a stream, or in a field of lilies. Whether indoors or outdoors, your chat room is an environment you create that is special to you, set up for the purpose of your comfort, inspiration, privacy, and safety. It's a place where you will share your innermost thoughts and concerns with your extraterrestrial helpers and then be willing to receive divine inspiration through the pep talk.

Here you will tell your coach all that is bothering or challenging you, in order to help clear your mind and prepare for the next step. You will verbally leave all your troubles on the doorstep of the universe. Then, your ET coach will assist you in strategizing your way to your next grand stage of life. But you can't be open to hearing a new strategy until you clear your mind of what's troubling you.

This is why determining the location of your chat room must take some thought. You will have to consider your lifestyle, who else lives in your house, and specifically where would be the most conducive place for you to create an environment of quiet, safety, and comfort.

When I first tried to contact the ETs from the comfort of my home, I chose a quiet room and set it up like a meditation room. Although I had been having ongoing ET contact, I had not yet learned to initiate it. For example, during one particularly startling experience, I awoke on some type of spacecraft staring in disbelief at a group of extraterrestrials. Instantly, we were telepathically communicating, but when I returned home, I wanted the process to continue. That's when I decided to start practicing the sessions that I describe here. They seem quite simple, and they are. But they're powerful. Remember, things don't have to be complicated to be transforming and miraculous.

As I first did, find a corner in your bedroom, garage, or office that you set up with pillows, blankets, chairs, and cushions. Decide if you'd like to use a chair, a bed, set up a place on the floor in a special room, or in a loft. Perhaps you have a cozy, private area in your backyard where there are flowers, trees, or any other setting that pleases you. This will be your comfy place that will serve as your sacred spot for contact. Adorn this special area with favorite items that will make you most comfortable. I had set up a special area in the family room, and I'd plan special sessions for when the house was empty.

Ultimately, your chat room creates a place where miracles happen. You will vibrate with your passion, hopes, dreams, and incredible vision for your future. It is your place of connection where you will initially meet for your coaching sessions.

What happens in your chat room? You will talk to extraterrestrials. With the ease that you dial a telephone or log on to a chat room on the Internet, you will learn to "log on" to the heartbeat of the universe.

The Meeting Place:
A Spaceship or
Your Bedroom?

Although the idea of having contact on a spaceship is exciting, if there is a lot of communication between you and the extraterrestrials, it will be difficult to remember it all while you're taking in the galaxy from their craft. So don't feel that your ET contact is not real if it begins in your chat room in your own home. This is the point of this book. Your home is where ET contact first begins, when you initiate your spiritual awakening. The *communication* between you and enlightened beings is what we are after. Remember, there is a reason your soul is seeking their mentoring. Often, metamorphs' initial ET contact begins with a conversation from the comfort of their own home.

Your first few practice sessions may include images, symbols, flashes of light, feelings, inner knowing, audible words, sounds, or sensations.

Communication between spiritual beings is not limited to spoken words. When beings evolve, they need say nothing to be understood by each other or you. We understand that when our guardian angels or other spirit beings visit us, they do not need to speak words that are transferred from mouths and then heard by our ears. Instead, the heart and the soul understand the communication. All who partake in this language of the soul can hear telepathic voices because the soul is all-knowing.

There's often a sound to the energies that begin to surround you as you open to contact. You may sense and hear crackling or buzzing. For this reason, it is best to establish a special room, free from distractions, people, noise, and discomfort, just for the purpose of initiating your initial "reunion."

The "Pep Talk" Will Deliver You Information and Inspiration That Will Help You Fulfill Your Soul's Blueprint

The other basic tool of telepathic coaching may not seem like a tool at all. You may agree that you'll need a chat room while you're learning to create a conducive environment in order to receive coaching. But you may not have considered that the content of that coaching serves as your daily dose of help leading you to greatness.

Think of this combination of tools in terms of a telephone. It is a two-step, two-directional process: your chat room is your telephone. It's the tool that facilitates the privacy and sense of safety and comfort needed for you to reach out and for ETs to reach "in" to your world. It's the space that you consciously create daily that helps prepare you for contact. Your chat room allows you to become ready to receive extraterrestrial coaching. Your chat room provides the venue from which your outgoing messages and requests are sent to the universe.

The pep talk delivered by telepathy is the second part of the process. It contains the incoming message that you are seeking, the help that will serve to change your life for the better. These pep talks will inspire you every day of your life. Pep talks deliver you information that will help strategize and navigate any course of action leading you to the fulfillment of your soul's blueprint.

Your Contract Serves As a Daily Reminder That Action Is Necessary to Implement a Dream

I'm going to ask you to enter into a contract with your as-yet-unknown ET coach. The contract asks you to begin regular, repetitive daily sessions of telepathic contact. Like any new method of communication, you have to practice in order to become proficient. For the next twelve weeks, use both tools—your chat room and the pep talk—to enter the universal stream and establish your alliance to the heartbeat of the universe. Once you enter into this contract, don't be surprised when your chat room turns into your car, office, grocery store, or airport and you realize that you're constantly connected to your coach. But even when your chat room extends out to incorporate "everywhere," you are agreeing to continue these structured practice sessions for at least twelve weeks.

Here's your contract. Please write this or retype this and fill in the blanks. Make several copies and post it where you will see it every day. Put one copy on your bathroom mirror and another on your refrigerator door.

I, _____, understand that I am under-
taking intensive, guided sessions with enlightened extraterrestrials. I commit myself to the twelve-week duration of
practice sessions.

I, _____, commit to daily sessions in my
chat room, during which I spend part of each session
purging my worries or concerns, and part of each session
receiving a pep talk.

I also understand that spiritual coaches will help me to
raise issues that have haunted me or bothered me. I,
_____, agree to take excellent care of
myself during this process of awakening spanning this
twelve-week period and agree to get adequate sleep, nutri-
tion, exercise, and pampering.

_____Date:_____
Signature

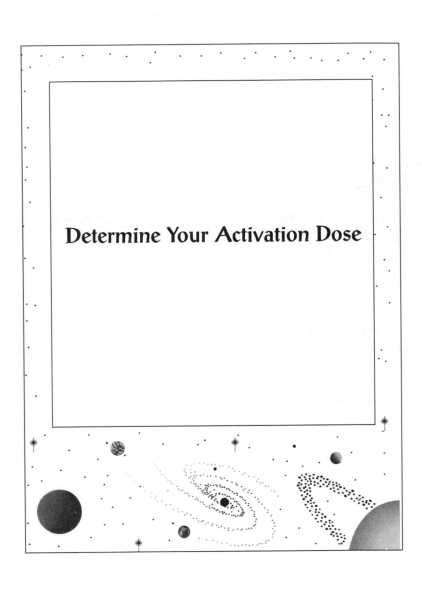

Determine Your Activation Dose

As you begin to set aside time each day for your practice sessions, you will have to determine how much of a daily time commitment will be required for you to jumpstart this process. Learning a language requires practice. Only you can determine how long you can and will be able to commit to your sessions. Generally, an hour daily is a good start. But some days, you may practice more. There may be other days where you skip practicing altogether. Your activation dose is a personal, spiritual commitment of time, and the frequency and the length of your sessions are made by an evaluation of your progress.

Some People Have Extraordinary ET Encounters, So Why Can't Most of Us?

Some people make connections to extraterrestrials that result in spontaneous physical healing, extraordinary personal development, and a general increase in many levels of functioning. Other people report that they've been kidnapped by unwanted alien intruders, victimized by uncaring strangers, and generally upset and violated by horrifying aliens. Why do some people report that encounters are wonderful and others insist they're victimizing?

Metamorphs who are winning at ET coaching understand the following:

- Metamorphs understand spiritual law that empowers each person to choose and attract the relationships that work best for them, whether or not those relationships are from this world or another.

- Metamorphs institute the "get help quick" system that includes the use of the chat room and pep talk. They have put into place structured practice sessions where they use telepathy to initiate contact with enlightened extraterrestrials.

- Metamorphs conduct all communications in the spirit of fun and potential enlightenment. They don't get persuaded by the culture to take everything so seriously. They don't get swept away by the cultural illusion that demands that we lose our laughter, sense of humor, and joy.

- Metamorphs refuse to adopt fear as a way of being. At the end of the day, metamorphs are better off, not worse, for having made contact.

- Metamorphs ask themselves two crucial questions:
    1. "In what area of my life do I need help?"
    2. "What have I come here to do?"

- Metamorphs plan to succeed.

How Will You Know
They're Enlightened ETs?

Telepathic content should always reflect the goodness of your coach. Trust yourself to know the voice of wisdom and love. If you get a message that tells you to go shoot the president, or attempts to tell you what to do or how to run your life, you are not communicating with enlightened beings!

There is a saying from the Bible that you will know the tree by its fruit. Remember this phrase always, and you'll know exactly with whom you're dealing.

If this makes sense to you, congratulations! You've mastered 99 percent of the source of most humans' objections to establishing otherworldly contact.

People are afraid of what's new, and they often use as an excuse to expanding their experiences the fear that if they reach out, they don't know what they'll get.

Simply close the door on those visitors from otherworldly realms you don't want to invite in. You are in charge. There is nothing to fear. If you don't feel a loving response, respond calmly and forthrightly with your verbal affirmation that you are interested in initiating contact only with enlightened beings who have come to help you with your highest purpose. Firmly state that all others should depart immediately. No debate, argument, or drama are necessary. You are in charge. You set the parameters. You are empowered.

You may be wondering if there are beings who *pretend* to be enlightened, but are not. Just as there are human beings who pretend to be one thing when they're really another, there are probably beings everywhere who fall along a wide spectrum of spiritual advancement. So here is the key again: You will recognize the tree by the fruit that it bears. Listen to their words. Feel the nature of the contact. You will know who they are by the quality of their message. If you sense negativity, control, or manipulation, simply end the conversation.

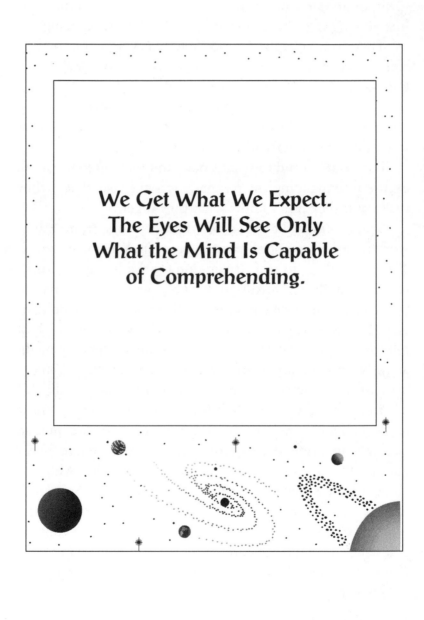

We Get What We Expect.
The Eyes Will See Only
What the Mind Is Capable
of Comprehending.

Many years ago, following a divorce, I had to take a serious look at my core beliefs about men. Until I changed my underlying beliefs that said men could not be trusted, untrustworthy men kept showing up to date me. Do you see how this works? Our inner beliefs dictate our outward events. If I believe that I'll never be rich, I won't be. If I believe that my cancer will kill me, it will. If I believe that I have no say in the type of worldly or otherworldly "people" who show up in my life, then I won't have a say. We get what we believe in. The eyes will see only what the mind is capable of comprehending. Our core ideas about a thing dictate an outer manifestation in our life. Remember, God answers beliefs. This is really what a prayer is.

By the same token, I do understand that many people cannot or will not subscribe to the notion that we all draw in to our experience what we need for growth at any certain time. Fifteen years ago, if you had told me that I had within me the power to change my situation or my relationship, I would not have believed you. In fact, I didn't believe that I had any power whatsoever to create the life or relationships that would work for me on any level.

So I don't expect everyone to accept the notion that all of our relationships—worldly or otherworldly—are of our choosing. It all depends upon where you are along the spectrum of awareness.

So now you are considering that your perceptions may determine the kind of relationships that you will attract. If we get what we expect, then you now understand why your perceptions of the universe will dictate what shows up in your experience. We attract that which we are and if we don't like what we're attracting, we can change who we are so that we can attract that which we say we want.

Your Soul Has an
Agenda to Know More
of Our Universe

I'm not suggesting that it's *my* idea for you to know extraterrestrials. It's yours, although you may not be consciously aware of it yet. Like my own soul's plan, ET contact may be part of your destiny, part of your soul's blueprint. This is something that is set up prior to birth, while we're on the Other Side, considering what we would like to do with our upcoming incarnation. I believe that is why you are here reading this. Your soul has led you to this page, asking you to begin.

Telepathy is not the only way to initiate ET contact. It's one way. If you resonate to the words here, it may be just what is needed. It's designed for those who are seeking encouragement to be all that they can be. When we tap into the energies of the higher realms, we can expect wondrous things to begin to happen. Telepathic communication with ETs is one way to get the ball rolling. When you are able to listen to the voices of extraterrestrials, you are setting up a spiritual platform from which you are then able to see them. If you have a burning desire to know more of our universe and the incredible beings that live there, then you too can establish relationships that will enhance your life immeasurably.

Best Results Are Achieved by Those Who Are Largely Healed

Because of the nature of otherworldly contact, I don't recommend these techniques for the squeamish, emotionally delicate, or psychologically impaired. Best results are achieved by those who are for the most part stable, emotionally and psychologically. It should be understood that I recognize that those who are mentally impaired may not be able to trust the voices they may hear. If you suspect that you have a mental impairment, attempting communication with otherworldly beings may disturb you further.

Find the Techniques
That Work Best for You

With the exception of your contract, the suggestions contained here are not meant to be rigid or concrete. The contract itself serves to remind you of your commitment to take your life to the next level. This will have to become engrained in your consciousness every day. Daily, you must recommit your decision to thrive and not just survive. You must make the time and space to use your chat room and the pep talk for them to play a bigger role in your life. But ultimately, you may find a different route to be assisted in connecting with our extraterrestrial neighbors. These portals are meant to help you get started, techniques that worked for me and for others in my classes and workshops.

Are You Ready for
a Daring Adventure?

Helen Keller once said, "Life is either a daring adventure or nothing." If this is true, then opportunity awaits us.

These practice sessions are designed for those who are leaders of the new dawn, who will be part of the first group of humans to establish contact with our otherworldly neighbors. History will one day show that someone got the ball rolling before everyone thought that it was possible.

This is the role that metamorphs play: *we are leading our species,* showing by our own example that we can become active members of our universal community.

The Nature of Your Beliefs
Will Either Limit You
or Launch You

If you insist that you're a victim in any way, you're still operating from within the cultural illusion. Such a perception will limit you and your experiences, and will limit and impact the quality of your life. It's your choice to choose an attitude that will end up serving you in the long run. Simply observe that empowered beings change their lives and their world. Those who believe they're incapable of empowering themselves do not.

In the spiritual realms, there is no level of difficulty when it comes to what we call miracles, or what appears to be magic. Enlightened beings do not perform magic when they appear and disappear at will, assist us in floating through the air, or help us to open to psychic gifts virtually overnight. We are not becoming something that we were not prior to contact. Instead, we are simply uncovering that which we already are: spiritual beings who have been asleep but who are now awakening. We will again be able to utilize the energies of the higher realms. We recognize that science does not have all the answers. Spirit does.

Love Will Unite You
through Telepathy

Divinity, and all those who are sponsored by divinity, work through the emotion of love.

One of my workshop students, Georgia Pearson, is now writing her own book about the extraordinary results she has achieved with this process. She senses that it's the power of love that makes it possible to unite telepathically. She says:

> I didn't think that this process was possible. I didn't know you could actually access otherworldly beings so easily and receive this type of enlightened guidance.
>
> I do these sessions every morning and I can feel how much more clearly my mental functioning is. This process has positively affected my mind to the point where I feel that I have a new level of brain functioning.
>
> My theory for why these sessions are so powerful is that the process induces a kinesthetic vibration that starts in my heart. It's their level of unconditional love that has had a palpable effect on me. Somehow, my ability to access my spiritual energy has been heightened. The energy exchange is somehow promoting a different energy throughout my body that has resulted in my life becoming "powered" in a new and different way. I know it all sounds so unbelievable. But now, I have an increased mental clarity and the solution to problems just falls into place. I have less worry and con- fusion. They're introducing a bigger, more fundamental energy that connects me to my source. Everything in my life just works so much better.

Your "First" Contact
May Not Be
Your First Contact at All

There's a very good chance that you've already met the ETs with whom you are seeking a relationship. You may have met them in your dreams, as part of an out-of-body experience, or when you were a child. Consider that telepathy will help initiate more conscious contact that stands to bring your life to a new level.

When you first become introduced to the group of ETs who await your readiness, there is a tremendous punch to your first greeting. Why? Because it may not be your *first* greeting at all. It is safe to say that most every one of us who is standing by, emotionally eager to begin receiving ET contact, has a deep connection already in place with the ETs. The single most empowering realization is to know this may be the case and that whatever contact you have will not be the first at all. Instead, it may be the contact that you first *remember* in this life.

You may imagine that you prefer extraterrestrials to knock on your front door and announce their arrival, but otherworldly phenomena don't work like that. This is why they are "other" worldly. Such phenomena are part of the higher realms and are therefore imbued with the quality of those realms, not our dense, physical world. As we've already discussed, contact can arrive in any number of ways and arrives "packaged" in various states and venues. You may not be emotionally ready to handle being brought aboard a craft, so you can begin with meeting extraterrestrials in your dreams or imagination. If this should occur, it is not a fantasy or wishful thinking. Your dream state and your imagination are preparing you for more. If you dream of ETs or if a burst of light explodes in your bedroom, consider yourself contacted!

Just as you may go for years without benefit of a family reunion with your great-aunts and uncles cross-country or overseas, when you do finally get together, there is tremendous joy in seeing your extended family again. Consider that your first ET contact is actually a relationship that has been re-established, and the contact may feel like a long-awaited family reunion. You may be surprised at the emotion of hearing from them again.

This is the reason that establishing contact is not nearly as difficult as you may think because you may already have had these reunions many times. It's even possible that you've had a reunion in this life—maybe last year, when you were a child, or last night—but you don't remember it. (For reasons why your memory may be blocked, see *Calling on Extraterrestrials: 11 Steps to Inviting Your Own UFO Encounters*.) The greatest difficulty in opening to ET contact is in addressing the resistance of the ego—not the soul—and of our cultural assumptions that deny our spiritual nature.

In reality, all you need to do is to get yourself out of the way, and your soul will do the rest. You will be able to listen to the communication that will be provided by your other-worldly family members because you are well equipped to do so and are destined to do so. We're all destined to do so as part of humanity's evolution. It's just that some of us have decided to be the first out of the gate, where we master this before the masses are able to. Then, we can demonstrate and prepare the rest of the planet in doing so, too. Pioneers establish a way and a route to a new world because they have the courage and fortitude to do so. You may be such a pioneer.

Once you have selected your chat room and done whatever is necessary to make it comfortable, you're ready to gather the items that will facilitate your ET contact through your chat room.

Action Items for Portal One:

- Select a special place that you will use for your chat room.
- Make it extremely comfortable.
- Give some thought to any unusual encounters you may have already had with otherworldly phenomena.
- Write down the beliefs that may be limiting your ability to achieve your goals through the practice of a telepathic connection to ETs.
- Write down the goals you may want to accomplish with personal coaching by ETs.
- Practice at least once a day, five days a week.

Surround Yourself
with Things That Cause
Other Things to Happen

Second Portal:

Prepping Your Chat Room

You're now ready to set up your chat room to include several items that will assist you in creating readiness for telepathic contact. These include:

- music that moves you to tears

- tape recorder

- jewelry of the universe (shell, rock, feather, crystal, flower, a carved box, etc.)

- the element of fire

- preparing with water

The items included might seem to have nothing to do with inviting UFO contact. But I emphasize how developing the ability to see, hear, feel, smell, and sense otherworldly phenomena means that you are increasing your sensitivity and thus expanding *spiritually*.

Let's discuss the first item on the list, music.

Music is an often-overlooked tool that will help in two different yet important ways.

Music Will Take You Away

Start your session by listening to a specific musical selection because it will help you to "buzz" with a high frequency as you begin to knock on the door of the universe. A universal law states that like attracts like. Use an extraordinary musical selection to help you to move to a higher vibration as preparation to reaching the higher realms. With the use of your special musical selection you will create a magical state of being and a divine state of readiness that will deliver you to the doorstep of the cosmos. There you will recognize that all things are possible.

Also, the way and manner that you allow yourself to be inwardly touched and moved by extraordinary music will help demonstrate to you the difference between listening and hearing. It's imperative to understand this distinction in order to learn telepathy. Choose just one or two songs that deeply touch you and create a tape or CD in which one entire side is made up of that one song. Choose an artist whose music resonates to a high vibration. My taste in music changes over time, but when I began my practice sessions many years ago, I used music from meditation tapes. You will know what works for you because of the way that you *feel* when you listen to it. Allow it to take you away. There's a great deal of incredible music available, offered as meditation or relaxation music. Experiment. Ask your friends for recommendations. This is an important step, determining the right and perfect selection of music that reaches your gut. Don't minimize it.

You can find a selection of meditation music, your favorite Beatles song, the Eagles, the music of Hilary Stagg, Enya, Cathy Bolton (www.cathybolton.com), Loreena McKennitt, or any classical music such as Mozart or Bach. Find any selection of music that touches your soul. You can visit a metaphysical bookstore and ask for suggestions. The goal is to select music that touches you deeply. You're not looking to be entertained by it, but to be moved by its sublime force.

Telepathy Involves Listening with Your Heart and Soul Instead of Your Ears and Mind

Hearing involves the process of internalizing auditory signals. But when we listen, we are listening with the "ears" of our heart and soul. This is how we detect telepathy.

Hearing is what you do when you watch television, hear ordinary conversation, or take in routine auditory input.

But when we *listen*, we are moved to passion. We *feel* seduced by an extraordinary moment in which we allow ourselves to be touched by sublime influences.

If you don't know what I mean by this, consider when you last listened to extraordinary music that elicited an emotional response. You were touched by what you heard. Perhaps even moved to tears.

When our sensitivities become profoundly affected, such moments offer us up to divinity and we are momentarily swept away by the profundity of life. While in this magical state of being, you will most easily listen to the ETs who are trying to make contact with you, because you will be in a state where your heart and your soul will do the listening for you. Magically, the process of telepathy will be induced.

Music Will Help You
Dance with
Higher Energies

After you have signed your contract that commits you to the work of these practice sessions, selecting the perfect musical selection that speaks to your soul is your next action step. You must not skip this part of the portal. Music is one of the most potent tools available in helping us to build the vibrations around us so that we can more readily dance with the higher energies of other worlds.

You will not use the music as background during your ET communication per se, since it may be too distracting. You will use music at the beginning of your sessions to help you get ready. Otherworldly dimensions are at your fingertips. Use your magical selection of music to dissolve a busy state of mind. Use music in the preparation of establishing contact. Once you are proficient at gaining entry to the otherworldly doorways, you will not necessarily need the music any longer, but you may choose it to enhance your sessions.

It's as though you are using a special energetic force field to deliver you someplace. The skier uses a ski lift to travel to the top of the mountain. In the same way, the metamorph can use music to deliver himself to the finer realms, having been lifted successfully up and out of the denser realm of our physical world. In the privacy and safety of your chat room, you will float on the music and allow it to open your chakras and deliver you to a sublime state of readiness. There are seven chakras, points located along the body considered as energy centers. One of them is the crown chakra, a point at the top of the head. Telepathy involves the opening of this energy center, which facilitates language being transferred from soul to soul. You may feel a strong buzzing or vibrating on your scalp or head which indicates that your crown chakra is opening and you're ready for the telepathic connection.

Why Is Music So Important to This Process?

Consider this potent excerpt by Don Campbell who wonderfully explains the power of music in his book, *The Mozart Effect: Tapping the Power of Music to Heal the Body, Strengthen the Mind, and Unlock the Creative Spirit*. He says:

What is this magical medium that moves, enchants, energizes, and heals us? In an instant, music can uplift our soul. It awakens within us the spirit of prayer, compassion, and love. It clears our minds and has been known to make us smarter.

Music is a holy place, a cathedral so majestic that we can sense the magnificence of the universe, and also a hovel so simple and private that none of us can plumb its deepest secrets.

Music helps plants grow, drives our neighbors to distraction, lulls children to sleep, and marches men to war.

Music can drum out evil spirits, sing the praises of the Virgin Mary, invoke the Buddha of Universal Salvation, enchant leaders and nations, captivate and soothe, resurrect and transform.

Yet it is more than all these things. It is the sounds of earth and sky, of tides and storms. It is the echo of a train in the distance, the pounding reverberations of a carpenter at work. From the first cry of life to the last sigh of death, from the beating of our hearts to the soaring of our imagination, we are enveloped by sound and vibration every moment of our lives. It is the primal breath of creation itself, the speech of angels and atoms, the stuff of which life and dreams, souls and stars, are ultimately fashioned. [Text from pp. 1–2 of *The Mozart Effect*, © 1997 by Don Campbell. Reprinted by permission of HarperCollins Publishers, Inc., Avon Books.]

Profound Music That
Emanates a High Vibration
which Touches You Deeply
Will Easily Carry You
to an Altered State
As Gently As the Wind
Carries a Hawk into
the Clear Blue Sky

The reason that you will only select one or two songs is that, as you enter an altered state, if the CD is moving from song to song, the disruption can be jarring. The same song replaying will be less distracting. In addition, don't record the song more than three times per tape or CD side. As you enter an altered state, you want the music to slowly drop away. After ten or twenty minutes, the music may actually feel disruptive, and you don't want to have to come out of your deep state to turn it off.

This portal will help you to use your special music as a doorway to enter otherworldly realms. Restful music that you determine has unique properties can be an extremely powerful tool.

To repeat, your mission is to find the music that inspires *you*, and then to make a tape or CD of just one or two songs to fill up one whole side of the CD, so that you can practice entering an altered state for approximately ten to twenty minutes. When you try using your recording, you may find that you need more time so you can record more music if needed.

Record Your
Practice Sessions

Get a tape recorder. From the first practice session, get into the habit of always using a tape recorder to record what you hear or sense. Don't assume that you'll remember what you've heard and that later when your session ends, you'll be able to recall it easily and write it all down. I have had several important telepathic sessions that I did not record and later regretted it. In one case, an answer to a long-standing problem had finally come through after months of asking. It took me by surprise and unfortunately my tape recorder was nowhere in sight. Due to my deep trance, I remembered little of the session. If only I had kept a record of the conversation. If you don't have a tape recorder, borrow one. If your chat room is located in a barn and there's no electricity, use a tape recorder with batteries. Spontaneously recording your impressions through the use of a tape recorder offers superior advantages. Don't begin your sessions until you are able to record them.

The Phenomenon Aspect
of Contact Is Interesting,
but the Personal Message
to You Can Change Your Life

When I first began to be contacted by extraterrestrials, there was a time when I was stunned to discover that I was floating through the air and being transported from a spacecraft to a group of ETs who were waiting for me on the "ground" below. I was in their world, not mine, and although it was incredibly fascinating, I did not have the benefit of being able to grab my tape recorder or writing pad. All I could do was attempt to take it all in while my mind was going a mile a minute. It was an incredible "conversion" experience in which my world turned upside down, but it was just a start. What was needed was for me to establish contact that could assist me in listening to them, listening to the voice of my own soul, taking time for my life, finding my purpose, and then change my life for the better.

I was provided tips about my health and it improved. I was assisted with my romantic choices and my relationships changed for the better. My chronic lack of financial abundance began to be transformed. Like any good personal coach, my ET coach helped me with every aspect of my life.

It always amazes me how swiftly and completely their message is "forgotten" just as soon as a session ends. While the communication is progressing, you may be certain that the clarity and intensity of their message will stay with you so that you can capture the message later. But don't be surprised if this isn't the case. Once your consciousness "returns" to the dense physical realm, the essence of the communication can evaporate in a heartbeat.

Ultimately, the mechanics of how you record the telepathy is less important than the quality of your connection. You may find that you prefer to relax and use a clipboard and pen or to sit at your computer keyboard. Your goal will be to find the process that works best for you and that minimizes the distortion and maintains the quality of communication.

Decorate Your Chat Room
with the Jewelry
of the Universe

Once you have identified what room you'll use as your chat room, and you have your music CD or tape prepared, it will help you next to fill your chat room with various energies. These energies come packaged as physical objects. What I mean by this is that ordinary objects that you can find in nature are actually balls of energy that you will be learning to sense. You're learning to increase your sensitivity. These energies are found in any animate or inanimate object, but the goal here is to choose objects from mother nature such as rocks, flowers, plants, or shells that you resonate to. I refer to these tools from nature as the jewelry of the universe. Have you ever considered that your favorite flower may grow elsewhere in the universe? When we surround ourselves with and use natural elements to help us connect to the universal heartbeat, we effectively *ride* those energies to higher realms. Jewelry of the universe are additional tools that uplift us. It is helpful to this process if we practice feeling the energies of a rock, shell, or crystal.

Since Spiritual Beings Are
Connected to Each Other
and to Everything in the
Cosmos, Then It Makes Sense
That We Can Develop the
Sensitivity to See, Hear
Sense, and Feel ETs
Just As We Learn
to Feel Other Energies

Spiritual growth can be accelerated when we increase our sensitivity and more fully recognize ourselves as spiritual beings living physical lives. If we can see a cloud, flower, crystal, or dolphin, for example, we can sensitize ourselves to *feel* their vibration. Conversely, when we can *feel* universal energies but don't yet *see* what's causing them, we are preparing ourselves to soon being able to see those energies manifest in physical form. Many of my students quickly learn to feel ETs' different energies and they're now practicing increasing their sensitivity in order to see them.

Spiritual growth can be understood as an increase in our awareness and sensitivity to that which connects everything. We may not consciously know why one room in our house is our favorite, but upon closer scrutiny, there may be plants or flowers in the room that uplift us. We may feel becalmed by the artwork, the furniture, or color scheme. In essence, in our chat room, we will choose to surround ourselves with things or tools that cause an increase in our awareness or sensitivity. This portal asks us to surround ourselves with things that cause other things to happen. The more aware we are of the life spark that is in a crystal or flower, then the more aware we will be of otherworldly beings who are shape-shifting around us.

Choose those things from our world that are bursting with a life spark, as you determine it. Whatever you like means it resonates with you. Choose a polished rock or shell that you found on the beach. Perhaps yellow roses make you feel happy when you smell or see them, so choose them as your jewelry. These tools will assist you in readying for contact and may include anything at all that you enjoy seeing, touching, smelling, or sensing. If there are daisies in your garden, put some in your chat room.

When We Connect
with the Energies and Elements
Provided by Mother Nature,
We're Using the Same Tools
That Shamans Use

Like the shamans, we can learn to connect with other energies and realms and we can use the same tools that they use to increase sensitivity and heighten connection to the One Source.

Not only will you place these items in your chat room in order to begin to feel how they impact the feel of the room, but once your telepathic sessions begin, you may begin to notice how the natural Earth jewelry surrounding you begins to change or move. Some students have reported that rocks or other items literally disappear during their sessions. One reader described how while cooking, the contents of the pot on the stove formed into a distinct face of an ET. I have had otherworldly beings arrive in my chat room and bring me an object from their realm. Once I was given a gift of a beautiful wood and bronze cross that I placed under my pillow. In the morning it was gone, but the joy from receiving it has stayed with me for a decade.

Select some of your favorite "touchy-feely" objects that are from the natural world. The list of possibilities is endless. You can have your favorite pet join you, as long as it remains still so as not to distract you. I have had pets nearby during sessions or following sessions and I have clearly "heard" their thoughts. As you can see, once you begin to practice these techniques, you will be delighted by how much fuller your life experiences become. Some possibilities are:

seashells
rocks
flowers from the garden
crystals, feathers, etc.
your goldfish, pet iguana, etc.
a wood carving
scented candles
strings of beads
your favorite tapestry

Many Extraterrestrials Are Really Universal Shamans

Evolved beings understand that the same energy runs through all there is. They recognize that the same energy makes a cloud, pony, extraterrestrial, or human. This is the basis for enlightened beings' ability to shape-shift since they work with energy and manipulate it to serve their desired experiences. As we increase our spiritual awareness, we're becoming shamans too. Since the same stuff of energy runs through it all, shamans pull from these energies, and feel a strong connection to it. Seashells, flowers, rocks, crystals, or even your cat can be perceived now to help you know your place in the universe. Your chat room is your special place on Earth that will connect you to others' special places on Earth. By decorating your sacred space with the lovely items from Earth's beaches, forests, or your garden, you are stirring your soul to remember all the different places it has been and to which you are connected.

Remember, your ET family may have known you from many different "locations." Those locations may have been on different planets or realms.

**Your Mission Today
Is to Honor the Role
You Are Playing
in the Location
That You're Playing It**

Churches, synagogues, and other houses of worship all are decorated with items of ritual and custom that assist a person to feel a connection to the One Source. You don't have to go to church to connect with your sacred self. You will do it right in your chat room, and today, tomorrow, or the next day, you'll expand that sense of sacredness to include anywhere in the universe.

Each of us has already lived hundreds or thousands of different lives. We have done so for the purpose of experiencing every facet of life imaginable. Many metamorphs have already had embodiments as Native Americans or as members of other wise tribes on other planets in which they were accustomed to accessing otherworldly realms through ritual, prayer, or tribal custom. Native peoples who are more closely attuned to the energies of Earth, can more easily feel all that is out there. This is a ritual in which we honor our present location as Earth people.

Shape-Shifting Is Possible
When You Know
We're All One

When you have selected your stone, shells, or crystals, soak them in a bowl of sea salt for one or two days, and then place them outside for another one or two days to clear them of other's energies who have handled them. After you have prepared them this way, do not allow anyone else to touch them since they will now be clear to resonate to your own electromagnetic vibrations. This is how you will begin to practice charging and re-energizing those seemingly inanimate objects around you so that you will do this to your own body.

Crystals, special stones, or any other earth jewelry helps to create the ambiance of your chat room's sacred space, both in your home and also in your mind. We're becoming aware of the magical nature of stones and crystals in order to awaken the magnetic energy within ourselves. We're becoming reacquainted with the powerful, all-knowing capabilities of our birthright because, like the crystals, etc., the human energy system is composed of the same electrons and protons that are electrical and magnetic. Crystals, humans, and evolved universal beings are all composed of the same electromagnetic energy. When we know this, then we can do as the shamans do: We can pass through walls, walk between worlds, and share in the magical nature of all that we are capable of, but have forgotten that we are.

Once I began to have physical contact with physical extraterrestrials, I began to easily travel all over the place and have out-of-body experiences in which I observed myself float through walls, fly over the city, visit friends' homes, all while my physical body remained in bed. Once we touch higher energies, we are returned to our empowered nature as spiritual beings. When we are living our birthright and feel and know ourselves to be spiritually empowered, then our lives really start to change for the better because the desires of the soul have been ignited.

Fire: To Light or
Cause to Glow
As If on Fire . . .
To Become Ignited

What will it take to trigger the burning desire of your soul?

This is one of the questions that you will ask and answer in your chat room, and by lighting a candle or starting a fire in the fireplace, you are igniting all the possibilities of creation.

Once you are touched by sublime universal energies, you will take measures to reconnect with that feeling every single day in your chat room. This is how individuals create a life of their dreams. They find a way to stay connected to their inspiration on a daily basis. By remaining inspired, they create miracles.

To symbolize this journey and the importance of staying ignited to your life's blueprint, I'm going to ask you to light your favorite scented candle in your chat room before you begin each session. Select a candle of the size, shape, color, and scent that pleases you.

Create a ritual of lighting your candle as you begin your daily session to remind you of what you are undertaking: You are inviting yourself to become ignited with your soul's passion. You are asking yourself to glow with the universal heartbeat so that others of the greater universe will aid you in your mission of growth. Your lit candle symbolizes how you will glow with the flame of your intention.

Ancient cultures understood the power of fire during their spiritual practices and rituals. Spiritual seekers everywhere, whether in houses of worship or during holiday celebrations, use the element of fire.

Fire Is Associated with
Purification . . .
It Burns Away the Dross
So That the Inner Beauty of
the Core Can Shine through
and One Can Rise from
the Ashes, Renewed

Fire is the metaphor for regeneration that will sponsor us as we recreate ourselves anew with the help of enlightened beings. There's a power that emanates from fire and you can use this element in reaching altered states of awareness. Although we may not recognize the reason, this is why houses of worship often are filled with lit candles.

Depending upon my home environment or the seasons, I use a fire in the fireplace or woodstove to conjure up universal elemental forces. In addition, I use scented candles in glass containers. The aroma is important and should be compatible with your sense of smell. If the scent annoys you, it will be a distraction. As you open to otherworldly contact of an enlightened nature, you will be learning to discern higher energies. When there is a candle lit in the room, or if there's a fire in the fireplace, are you able to feel anything different?

ET contact involves becoming comfortable in sensing higher energies. Working with physical tools such as music, fire, water, and the natural gifts of the Earth helps us detect these and delivers us to the higher frequencies.

Water Is the Great Neutralizer and Purifier

Water is used in baptismal ceremonies to symbolize the cleansing of our past and our emerging into a rebirth. Water will help prepare you for your session.

As you immerse yourself in water, imagine all the cares and worries of the day washing away. Not only will this imagery help you relax, but warm baths are essential in clearing the chakras. I often take a warm bath twice daily and I bathe or soak in a hot tub, or swim in the ocean or lake before an important session. If you like, you can also begin the first prayer of your session while in water.

Your prayer is merely your words spoken out loud in which you claim your highest destiny. That claim is for yourself and others with whom you come into contact. Remember, metamorphs are embarking upon a spiritual adventure. We understand that our words will set up our actions, which will sponsor the experiences that show up.

Any ritual involving water is a potent environment in which to incorporate the words of our choice that will spark our higher path. You can say any prayer of your choice, or any words that propel you to a higher state of being. If like attracts like, then your music, mood, and joyous feelings of connection will contribute to the quality of your connection.

We Erroneously Believe
That We Need Some
Extraordinary Blanket
of Protection When We
Establish Connections to
Our Extraterrestrial
Neighbors, Protection That
We Rarely Attempt to Invoke
When We Go About
Our Daily Lives Here
with Each Other

One frequently asked question has to do with protection. People are worried that they'll open themselves up to nasty critters of the universe and they won't be able to get rid of them. They want to know what special exercise they should do in order to stay safe.

My answer is that as spiritual beings, we are always safe, although we rarely believe that we are. But if you're more comfortable in practicing a ritual of "safety" by all means do so. My suggestion is to continue to invoke any practice, ritual, prayer, or incantation that you practice when you set out in *this* world.

The Quality of Your
Demeanor As Expressed
through Your Thoughts,
Words, and Actions
Will Determine Your
Experiences in All Areas,
Whether Those Experiences
Are in This World
or Another

Suppose that there are no more risks in venturing out into the cosmos as there are in driving to the mall? Yet an unbelievable amount of media hype has us believing otherwise.

When it comes to our universal relationships and experiences with ETs, suddenly we're timid. Even when we personally know of many others who have been killed, maimed, or injured while driving cars, playing sports, or pursuing daily activities, we don't become sobered into the issue of "protection" like we do when we say that we want to talk to extraterrestrials.

The practices and rituals that I've included (music, jewelry of the universe, fire, water, and prayers of intention) are for the purpose of helping us to reach a higher frequency and to begin to feel the universal heartbeat. Extraterrestrials are also part of Mother Nature and the universal heartbeat. By recognizing that we get what we expect and that like attracts like, we can use whatever tools, prayers, rituals, or practices that help us to increase our faith and energetic frequency.

However, if you ask me if I think that there are specific challenges in playing a bigger role in the universe, I'd answer yes. Do I think that a spiritual initiate will be tested and challenged and asked to grow and stretch in becoming all that he or she can be? Yes, yes, yes. Is this process of becoming a spiritual initiate—a metamorph—easy? No, but it's worth it.

You Will Be Guided by
Your Divine Helpers
Because This Is
a Divine Process.
The Help You Need Along
the Way Will Be There
If You Trust That It Is.

Personally, I'm not satisfied in living a mediocre life. I'm called to push the envelope, explore the edges of the new frontier. I'll never be satisfied in spending my life watching television and paying the bills. I want more for my life and yes, I've been tested and strengthened and prepared for a bigger role. But that's a role I've chosen. If you want to play a bigger role, then yes, the bigger role you play will carry bigger challenges.

So are there risks? Yes, but not the ones that you've assumed. The flaming arrows that are always pointed at you will stop those who are not committed to spiritual growth. It's much easier for humans to stay disempowered than to become powerful spiritual beings consciously aware of their place in the universe. Remember the flaming arrows that I spoke of in the introduction? Let's repeat them here:

- self-doubt
- others' fear of what we are attempting
- others' criticism
- our own cautiousness
- fear of the unknown
- belief in the cultural myth that has us believe we're unsafe and disempowered

These flaming arrows are pointed straight at you. Will you succumb to them? They do not have to prevent your spiritual expansion, but they often do. So if you want to say a prayer of protection, by all means say it. If you want to read from the Bible, pray the rosary, eat garlic, by all means do it.

But then, let go and let God.

**Ultimately,
Contemplating the Ideas
Here, and Practicing
the Techniques
Will Help You to Raise
Your Vibration
to the Extent That It Will
Render Negativity Inert**

When we are vibrating with a positive demeanor, we attract the same positive energies from everywhere in the universe. Your attitude becomes your best protection since your attitude about life in general determines the experiences that you call to yourself.

Action Items for Portal Two:

- Find and prepare a musical selection that moves you to tears.
- Buy a recording device and extra tapes and batteries, and make sure it works properly.
- Select an object or objects from the natural world, "jewelry of the universe."
- Buy some candles that please you.
- Select and prepare your water ritual.

You're now ready to begin your first practice session!

**Your Chat Room Becomes
an Environment in Which
You Practice Energy-dense
Sessions That Deliver You
to the Door of the Universe
through the Elevation
of Your Vibration**

Third Portal:

Getting Started

You're now ready to begin to supplement your daily activities with a dose of energy-raising practices that make it possible to connect with enlightened extraterrestrials. This connection between you and the ETs can continue for the rest of your life. Here's what you will be doing as part of this portal:

- Make an appointment with yourself for your first session.
- Settle in your chat room and get extremely comfortable.
- Start your music.
- Purge every worry on the doorstep of the universe where it belongs.
- Bring yourself to a state of relaxation.
- Push the "record" button on your tape recorder.
- Repeat out loud whatever you hear, feel, sense, see, or smell.
- Ask questions, repeat out loud any response you "hear" no matter how you may want to judge it or deny it.

Send a Clear Message
to the Universe
That You're Serious
about Making Contact

Plan to schedule at least an hour with yourself for your first session. Your chat room is quiet and free from distraction. Remember to turn off the phone.

In the early days of your communications, it will help if you plan your sessions for when no one else is at home. Although you may be able to sequester yourself in a room, the differing energies of others in the same building can be distracting in the early stages and may impact the quality of your connection. Once you become more proficient at this, you should be able to connect even when there's a group of people in the same room.

Once you have the house to yourself, sequester yourself in your chat room and lock the door so no one accidentally interrupts you.

Once you have bathed and lit candles or started a fire in the fireplace, arrange your cut flowers, seashells, crystals, or feathers next to you, and have at the ready your instrument for capturing the communication. If you can't get a tape recorder, choose a writing pad and pen. Select a pen that glides easily and be certain that the pad of paper is firm enough to place in your lap. Use a hard surface such as a clipboard underneath the pad if it's helpful.

For your first few practice sessions, you'll be experimenting a lot. To set yourself up for success, do not begin this process if you're tired. If you are, build time into your session to first take a nap.

Telepathy between the Species Is the First Step towards Universal Participation

Remember, this process involves building up the character of your vibration so that you can interact with extraterrestrials who exist at a higher vibration. You're starting out on an adventure into the new frontier so you should feel excited about what you're undertaking. Beginning your session when you're refreshed will also help you from defaulting to doubt, which is a natural part of the opening process.

Fatigue is a strong inhibitor in receiving a quality communication. If you are physically or emotionally exhausted before you begin your session, you are more likely to experience mental distortion during this process. "Dancing" with the higher energies can exhaust you. You'll know you have made contact if, in the early stages, you can barely stay awake, which is why so many metamorphs report falling asleep when initial contact is made. Even after doing sessions for years, I prefer starting before 8:00 P.M. when I'm fresh.

Over time, you're being prepared energetically to withstand, acclimate to, and then thrive within these varying energies. At first it may be difficult to sustain communication for more than a few minutes without exhausting yourself. But after some exposure to the higher energies, your vibration will be strengthened.

Now, choose a position, either sitting in a comfortable chair or lying down on your back slightly inclined with pillows under your knees. Many experts on channeling have offered different advice on how to learn to channel. But this is not classic channeling so I don't subscribe to any one particular viewpoint as the right or best method. The ETs with whom you are telepathically communicating are alive in the physical form; they are not disembodied spirits who have crossed over.

You are going to discover the way and manner that is easiest for *you* to hear them. Your ongoing guidance will hopefully continue with *them* becoming established as your mentors. Once you establish communication, they can assist you in recognizing the best manner for your ongoing contact.

The early years of my ET contact involved face-to-face contact where my physical body was levitated onto their craft and I traveled to their world. But as the years went by, my life entered a different stage in which I wanted to stay more in my own realm but continue to communicate with them. I learned to use telepathy while remaining on Earth.

When I began communicating with them in my home or garden, I would initially start out by sitting in a chair, but I was unable to progress very far with my relaxation techniques. I then moved to a lying position where I could more easily relax, which allowed me to hear them. Later, I moved back to a chair because I had learned how to relax and to connect. Sitting upright better facilitates a strong connection and I became adept in listening to their communication.

For best results as you progress with telepathy, it's better to sit upright with your spine erect. But in the beginning, you're still learning what telepathy "sounds" like, so your ability to relax completely will help you to get started. Many people aren't able to fully relax while they're in a sitting position, so after you become confident with this process, you can shift to an upright position.

Once you have chosen your position, gather beside you within easy grasp your CD or tape player and your communication instrument (tape recorder, writing pad, pen, keyboard with a long extension cord), your crystals, shells, your favorite blankets and pillows, and a box of tissues.

If you're using a tape recorder, make certain you have already done a test—that you have fresh batteries, and that the clip-on microphone battery is new. The tape should be in place and the recorder ready to use. Do not begin until you have completed a successful test of the equipment. Do a test before you begin a session. During your session, take care not to cover it with a blanket or pillow. If you are using a tape recorder without a clip-on microphone, be sure you have the volume turned up and that's it's close to you.

If you're lying or sitting, place the tape recorder next to you rather than having it in contact with your body. If you're using a clip-on microphone it should already be clipped to your shirt. The ETs' energy, as it moves through your body, can "fry" a tape recorder in one session, so you can reduce wear and tear by keeping the recorder out of direct contact with your body. Remove your watch and keep it away from your body. Many of my students have had expensive watches break during a session.

I use a clip-on microphone that enables me to keep the tape recorder at arm's length. Do not hold the recorder in your hand and do not place the recorder on your lap. The energy surges will cause it to malfunction.

If this happens, as silly as it sounds, I place the recorder in the refrigerator for the night. I then allow it to return to room temperature before using it again. I have had success with this odd method of restoring electronic equipment to a state of functioning after an evening of ET zapping!

You're Embarking upon the Greatest Adventure of All Time

In case you're wondering why I suggest having a box of tissues within easy reach, you may be surprised at how emotional you become when you make your first contact with your long-lost friends. I've known grown men to cry like babies as they joyfully reconnect to extraterrestrial compatriots whom many of us have been in touch with since the beginning of time.

In addition, your sessions may include some of the most honest, heartfelt discussions you've ever had and those can be emotional. Having tissues within reach will allow you to work through sessions in which you may become upset.

You want to be extremely comfortable. The temperature in the room should be to your liking. You can do the session outside if the weather is comfortable and there are no distractions. I've had many wonderful sessions outside under the trees.

Wear loose, comfortable clothing. Often, when contact begins, you may become cold or hot. This does not indicate that you're fraternizing with the devil or with evil forces. When the human body begins to be exposed to otherworldly energies, there is naturally a period of adjustment as we acclimate. In case you become cold, it's helpful to have a blanket nearby. In the early days I would always begin with a blanket on me, so that I wouldn't become distracted later in covering myself to get warm.

There should be nothing rushing you. Ideally, there is no deadline looming over you in the next hour or so. You're a free agent, ready to embark on an adventure of a lifetime. It's natural to feel excited and be eager to get results, but the challenge will be to first reach a state of complete relaxation while you are simultaneously excited to connect with ETs. This will not be an easy task if your mind is going a mile a minute.

Allow Your Music to
Open the Portal for You

Start playing your selection of music. If it helps, reread the quote I provided earlier about the magical process of music. Although you may not understand the power of music to raise your vibration and carry you away, trust in its potency to do so. Have a copy of the quote on your lap and read it before your session for inspiration.

Settle back and begin to feel the music wash over you. You have already established that your particular musical selection can and will carry you to a state of personal triumph or bliss, so you will be repeating that process now. Find the right volume that will assist the music in reaching you deeply. Now close your eyes and relax.

If You Feel Blocked
or Distracted,
Purge Every Care
on the Doorstep
of the Universe

Some people are not able to make progress with their session because they're upset about something. If this is the case, you may need to begin by telling the universe what troubles you. Trust that someone is listening. Don't hold back. This is your chance to be honest. That's what a coach is there for. This is your opportunity to speak out loud and tell your coach of the details of your heartache. What is eating at you? What are you afraid you will never accomplish? What is your greatest worry? What has you lying awake at night? Who are you not able to reconcile with? What is preventing you from starting over?

This is the stage of your "telephone call" in which you admit to yourself and your coach all that is troubling you. Don't be surprised if you begin to cry. Allow whatever emotions you have to surface. It's healthy and necessary to purge your emotions to a trusted confidante.

Use your music to help you get in touch with whatever is up for you. This is an opportunity you've called to yourself to begin to heal. This part of your session can be very powerful

Believe in a power greater than yourself. You will be assisted always in overcoming any challenge that exists. There's no problem too big that cannot be healed by divine intervention.

Speak clearly so that your tape recorder can pick up your voice. Speak forthrightly as though you believe that they can hear you. Never mind if you feel silly, embarrassed, or don't know whether or not ETs are actually there. As the saying goes, "fake it until you make it." What this means is that you may have to go on faith until you develop more confidence in the process.

Bring Yourself to
a State of Bliss

If you did not need to purge negative feelings, start the music and close your eyes. If you used the first part of your session to purge, now is the time to move to the next stage. Keeping your eyes closed begin to think of things that bring you great joy. Imagine how things would be if you were living your fantasy. The sky's the limit. Allow yourself to play with your highest idea of how things would be if you were living your bliss.

Imagine that it's not only possible that you begin to thrive—not strive—but that the soul of the world depends upon you achieving your life's goals. What would be your right livelihood? Your relationships? Where would you live?

Through this exercise you are using your dreams to lift you up, remembering that dreams can come true, if you only believe. The goal here is to allow yourself to feel *wonderful.* With your music playing and your imagination taking an exquisite tour of your highest idea for your life, you'll begin to resonate a certain type of vibration.

Now take yourself higher still. Allow yourself to create in your imagination the way you would like to look, the financial abundance that you would share with those you love. Picture your health in a state of vibrancy.

Replace Your Imagination
with a Peaceful Void

When you reach a state of emotional pleasure, let your thoughts dissipate. To help you empty your mind, imagine the hand of a stopwatch in the straight-up position of sixty and imagine the hand moving counter-clockwise as the hand counts down from sixty to zero. As the hands slowly sweep around the face of the clock, with every passing five seconds you are becoming more deeply relaxed. With every passing second, your mind begins to let go of all its thoughts. Allow your thoughts to dissipate, until you're peacefully, fully in the moment.

If your thoughts begin to start up again, begin the process again and imagine the sweeping hands of stopwatch counting you down to emptying your thoughts. If you hear noises outside, the dog barking, or the faucet dripping, just allow them to be part of your background. Use them to help you go still deeper into relaxation.

Once you have relaxed thoroughly as a result of your music and/or whatever method you choose, with your eyes closed, slowly reach for the recorder next to you and turn off the music. If you're lying down, sit up a bit and pull a pillow up behind you so that you are at least sitting somewhat upright. Ideally, you will have your tape recorder and your tape player that's playing your music within easy reach and you will have memorized where all the buttons are so that you can activate them by feel, without needing to open your eyes. Ideally, you'd have two tape players, one to hold your music and the other to record your sessions.

Imagine That You Are
Plugging-in to
the Electrical Outlet
of the Universe

Now imagine the scalp of your head becoming charged with electricity. You may feel a strong buzzing sensation and you may also hear a crackling as your crown chakra opens and you become ready to receive communication. With your eyes closed, you may "see" a hue or color in your mind's eye. Allow it to expand and envelope you.

If you are like me, your head will begin to "crackle" and move slowly on its own. Allow it to do so freely. If any part of your body twitches or moves on its own, don't be alarmed. Simply enjoy the sensations and hear the crackling energies surround you. Know that you are making real progress.

Key Points:

- Your chat room becomes an environment in which you practice energy-dense sessions that deliver you to the door of the universe through the elevation of your vibration.

- Risk exposing your deepest worries through your purging sessions.

- Don't judge what you hear, even if you suspect that you're making it up. Continue with the process despite your doubt.

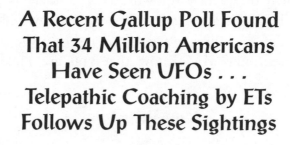

**A Recent Gallup Poll Found
That 34 Million Americans
Have Seen UFOs . . .
Telepathic Coaching by ETs
Follows Up These Sightings**

Fourth Portal:

The Pep Talk

Extraterrestrials are visiting Earth, awaiting our readiness to connect with them. Many people have reported seeing their crafts in the sky, including former President Jimmy Carter, John Lennon, Walter Cronkite, and astronaut Edgar Mitchell. Other people report having had dreams of ETs.

You've completed a session of purging and/or you've begun to fully relax. You're now ready for the pep talk. This is the part of the session in which you will actively listen with your heart and soul to the inspiration provided to you by enlightened beings.

With your eyes closed, imagine enlightened extraterrestrials standing by, awaiting your first communication. This group may already have a long-standing soul connection with you.

The ETs may be physically located in their realm—or right next to you in your room, although you don't yet see them. They may take on any number of appearances. Imagine that you and they had agreed long ago, prior to your birth, that you would eventually begin this process with them. Now the long-awaited day is finally here!

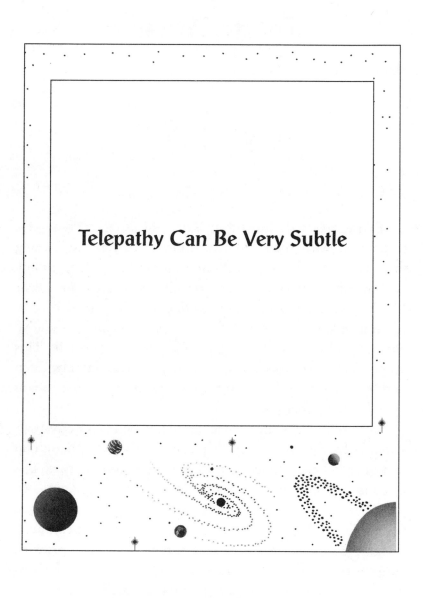

Telepathy Can Be Very Subtle

You may begin to hear words or an idea that seems to drift into your consciousness with the subtlety of a warm summer breeze blowing across your face. When you first detect the telepathic voice, it may be so subtle that you dismiss it as your imagination. Don't. Even if you're highly skeptical, suspend your disbelief and allow miracles to happen.

If you think that you've heard just one word, repeat that word aloud, and listen to the next word that will be provided immediately following the first word. As you learn this process, the ETs will often deliver one word at a time as you're growing more comfortable. Your job is to trust in the process and accept that one word at a time that's being provided.

It may take you several minutes to receive one complete sentence. Be patient with yourself in the same way that you'd be patient with a toddler who is learning to speak.

Sometimes you'll receive a message or concept that comes to you in a clump of emotions or one idea that seems to come at you in a bundle of words mixed with ideas. If this happens, relax, and simply describe the feelings or the idea that seems to be imparting itself to you. Take your time, and remember that you're learning and practicing. With practice, you'll be able to talk and listen more fluidly and with more speed.

Allow incoming words, images, or feelings to impress themselves on you. Do not censor yourself. If you see an image of a key, try to sense the feeling that accompanies the image. Are they congratulating you for using the key of willingness to finally establish this long-awaited contact with them? If you see an image of a heart, are they sending you love? Can you see an image of them?

Telepathy Is Like
a Gentle Touch,
Not a Scream

Detecting this subtle voice the first time is the hardest part of this process. But believe me when I tell you that as soon as you recognize it, you'll be off and running. You're learning to detect a very light touch as expressed through words and symbols.

To repeat, in the beginning, you may only hear a single word or phrase. When you do—even if you think you might be imagining it—repeat what you hear out loud. Often, you will not be able to hear any additional words until you first repeat what you've been given. The tendency is to want to wait until you receive an entire sentence or thought or phrase before you commit to repeating what you have. Instead, commit to accepting what you get in the way that you get it.

ETs Will Adjust the Style and Vocabulary to Suit You

For example, if you think you hear, "Hello, welcome," repeat these words and wait patiently for what comes next. Your tape recorder will be recording you. When I first started these communications, it was a slow exchange of words that increased in speed over time. The first sentence I received took twenty minutes to repeat out loud. Be patient with yourself and simply take each word individually as it comes to you. Do not judge or analyze it. Allow the words to come and repeat them aloud, no matter how much doubt you have that what you're hearing is authentic.

Expect the ETs to be wonderfully humorous and to use colloquial phrases and terminology as experienced by you in your own language. Remember, they're enlightened and evolved. When you were a toddler, your parents used the words and phrases that were familiar to you, and adjusted their style and communication to suit you.

Evolved ETs also take into consideration everything about you. Just as you might understand that a smile or laughter can transcend all barriers of ethnicity and language, telepathic conversation does too. They will communicate to you in words and phrases that are familiar to *you*.

My experience, and the experience of many others who have begun this process, is that ETs are warm, witty, and *funny*. They understand that you may be nervous and doubtful, so they will assist in helping you to feel more comfortable emotionally. This is not your imagination! If they banter with you playfully, record what you hear and know that the communication is really happening.

A Telepathic Connection
to You Will Be Celebrated
throughout the Universe

You have no idea how much excitement there is on their end and how much preparation has been going on behind the scenes, probably years or even decades, before you finally sit down to listen to them.

For days, months, years, or decades, your extraterrestrial coaches have been slowly exposing you to their differing levels of electromagnetic frequencies. They may have been visiting you for years in the middle of the night, in your dreams, or when you were a child. Now you are going to get together again so there's a lot of excitement and anticipation at their end. The first time I made telepathic contact from home I was so overjoyed I sobbed for quite a while. I could feel their joy too.

If you start to remember images of experiences long past, or dreams that you once dismissed, remember that none of this is coincidence. Certain humans have long been prepared to make ET contact a regular part of their human life at this time on the planet. Finally your soul blueprint can get underway. Congratulations for having the courage to begin the process!

The "Side-Effect" of Receiving a Pep Talk Is Self-Doubt

As you begin to repeat or write down the words that you hear, it's time for you to hold in your consciousness the reality of the most "harrowing" side-effect of successfully receiving ET coaching. When your pep talk begins, you won't believe it. Self-doubt may kick in so strongly that you'll want to abort this process. Don't.

Humans have a tendency to deny their spiritual nature. With the constant influence of the ego and intellect, it's easy to denounce, ridicule, minimize, or just plain forget evidence of divinity manifesting in our life. Receiving and understanding the pep talk is commonly inhibited by our strong cultural tendency to deny it once it's begun. We instinctively avoid that which we don't fully understand.

Just As You Begin to Make Real Progress, Self-Doubt May Plague You

One of the most difficult aspects of successfully communicating with extraterrestrials is the self-doubt that is generated the moment you begin listening to them. You may wonder if you're going crazy, fraternizing with the devil, or imagining it all.

The moment you connect, self-doubt often becomes your constant companion because the ego won't approve of your developing relationships with evolved beings. At this point you may talk yourself out of continuing. You'll wonder why, if ETs exist, they don't just beam you on board their craft so that you can become a real believer. Just as soon as you connect, you may think of every excuse possible to avoid continuing the process. Telepathic communication, you decide, is not tangible enough for you to develop confidence that you've actually connected to them.

The Intellect Refuses
to Believe in
the Telepathic Process

I've got news for you. It wouldn't matter if an alien stood next to you at the dinner table. You'll still have to pass through the hell of your own self-doubt. It comes with the territory. Even if extraterrestrials were to fly you on board their craft next Tuesday afternoon, and you could witness an incredibly fascinating glimpse of their world, the second your feet touch back down in your own front yard, you'll stop, scratch your head, and say, "Did I just *imagine* that?" And if it happens again on Friday night when you're given a special message, or a special task to do—no matter how wonderful, or important, or life-altering the contact was— when you return to your kitchen you'll ask, "Did I just imagine that as part of my wishful thinking?"

And then on Saturday morning you'll awaken after a night of the most amazing light show in your bedroom and later that morning you'll be trying to make sense of the coffee maker while you rub your head and gaze out the window, wondering if you've taken leave of your senses, or at the very least, if perhaps you imagined some of it.

This is the question that, if you're not asking it of yourself, every person you mention your experience to will ask for you. *Because the intellect just cannot believe it.* The ego insists that science has all the answers, and if anything extraordinary is happening, it has to be happening to somebody *else,* or not at all. It's crucial to understand the nature of self-doubt and the role the intellect plays to sabotage you as you begin returning more fully to your spiritual nature.

If You Understand the Nature of Self-Doubt, You Will Be Unstoppable

So, my wonderful and courageous new friend, if you do nothing else, or remember nothing else, remember this: If you indulge your self-doubt and continually defer to the ego, you will delay your spiritual growth and delay ever fully returning to your spiritual nature.

Believe in the Profundity
of Your Experiences

This may be the single most important reason that you have found this book: for me to remind you to believe in your role as a member of a greater universal family. It's all right to believe that you have been contacted. It's okay to simply go with this process and surrender to these practice sessions and allow yourself to see what happens for a twelve-week period.

Ironically, the Self-Doubt
That Is Generated
Is Often Your Best Indicator
That You're Making Progress

Something must be happening to trigger all that intellectual analysis. Truly crazy people seldom question themselves. The most dysfunctional and psychologically splintered among us rarely have serious moments of introspection and self-analysis. You're probably not crazy if you're afraid that you are, although it's possible to both open to ET contact and to also be in need of some sort of counseling. Sometimes ET contact will even cause you to know that you indeed should seek further help of the human variety, not because you're seeing aliens, but because the ETs have come to encourage you to become fully healed.

For many people, it will be helpful to liken the "side-effect" of self-doubt to the side-effect of sore muscles when an athlete trains hard for an upcoming competition. The athlete understands that he will have certain physical symptoms after undertaking the rigors of his given sport. After a long day of working out or competing professionally, the athlete expects to have some soreness. It's part of the process of toning the body and preparing for the skill to master a sport.

Rather than allowing muscle soreness to dampen his enthusiasm, the well-trained athlete understands that the physical sensations that occur as a result of conditioning the body indicate that conditioning is in fact taking place.

Like the Athlete, Metamorphs
Also Have a Set of Signature
Symptoms That Begin to
Emerge As They Get
Underway with the
Training of Their Own Mission
Involving ET Contact.
Those Signature Symptoms
Come Packaged As Self-Doubt.

If ever there will be an opportunity to begin doubting what you are hearing, seeing, or perceiving, ET contact offers a plethora of opportunities to second-guess yourself. It just comes with the territory. Until our culture more readily accepts the possibility of daily and routine contact by extraterrestrials, humans will always have a small voice in their mind that mirrors the greater cultural voice, questioning the veracity of their perceptions.

As metamorphs, we are still immersed in our culture although we are attempting to break out of it. But until you do, you will not have much success with ET contact if you don't initially recognize the wall of self-doubt that you may have to address as you begin to make progress.

Instead of attempting to ignore it, deny it, or be angry at it, you will be well-served if you simply recognize self-doubt as part of the mission of your ego and as the price that you have to pay as you proceed with your soul's agenda. It's truly the price of admission. All in all, it's a small price to pay in the long run because if you stay with this process, one glorious, magical day you'll notice that the majority of your self-doubt has vanished.

When You Understand
That Your Ego Is Not
All-Knowing—but Thinks That
It Is—You'll Be Able to
Maneuver Patiently around It
As You Would Maneuver
around a Rebellious,
Indignant Teenager

If self-doubt begins to scream at you, just hold on to your center; hold on to your spiritual understanding of the nature of divinity and allow the mind to scream in protest. The teenager of your protesting ego may not become quieted for a long time, but your soul will know that it cannot be allowed to diverge from its path by the doubts of the ego. Don't stop your session.

So to sum up, self-doubt is part of this process—until it's not. You might as well make friends with the voice of your self-doubt, because its protest will attach itself to you as soon as you begin to make progress. The ego wants to be in charge. It wants you to listen to *it*. When you threaten replacing it with a higher authority, it will kick, scream, and protest, hoping that you will abandon the process of relating to your otherworldly family members. Just know that the manner and style of its protest reflects as your own self-doubt and if you stay with your spiritual expansion, doubt eventually dissipates.

So I tell you this to prepare you beforehand. You are likely to abandon the process of preparing for contact if you are not prepared for the barrage of self-doubt that will set in just moments, hours, or days after completing your first transmission. That's the way that it works and why the ego's protests are so effective with less committed individuals. That's why I stated earlier that your burning desire for ET contact *will* ensure your success. Without it, you may give up just when you begin to make real progress.

My suggestion is to proceed daily with your practice sessions and as soon as you begin to doubt yourself, you'll be able to refer to this passage and say, "This is what Lisette was talking about."

**Self-Doubt Stops
Most Metamorphs.
Will You Let It Stop You?**

One sure-fire way that you will know you've made contact is by the way you will *feel* when you hear their first telepathic words. (Go ahead and cry. Your tissue box should be right by your side.)

This is why I had you first listen to music that moved you emotionally to your core so you will remember the similarity when your soul seems to be deeply stirred. This same feeling often accompanies your first telepathic session. Your *soul* will hear and feel their words, but your *mind* will doubt the words. Before too much doubt sets in, you'll allow yourself to recognize that indeed you do *feel* a connection with a power greater than yourself. And bingo! You've been contacted!

Initially, as you become more comfortable communicating this way, it may feel like it's your own thoughts that are being produced, not ET dialogue. Despite your doubt, begin to record what you hear anyway and respond to them with your own words. If you're using a writing pad, write down the communication and your response. If you're using a tape recorder, be certain that it's in the "record" position. Experiment with stating the words aloud and repeating the words you hear aloud.

Sometimes the ideas or suggestions that become part of the pep talk are not similar to what your own imagination would have come up with. You'll soon recognize that someone else is in fact doing the talking. On the other hand, your ET coach may discuss something about which you've been long considering. Where do you think the idea may have come from? Divinity reaches us through our imagination.

Do not judge what you are hearing. Or more accurately, allow the mind to judge all it wants but ignore it and proceed anyway. You may have an ongoing internal dialogue that questions if you are imagining what you think you're hearing. This is typical of the early process of the pep talk. Ignore your doubts and continue with the process.

One of the first questions that you pose to them may be "Who are you?" or "Where are you?" If you hear or feel no response, try different questions, questions that are less threatening to the intellect. No matter how ridiculous the response seems to be, just allow it to come through and continue with the dialogue. Record what you hear.

Until you become proficient, avoid asking questions that carry a lot of charge. Your first session is not the appropriate time to ask if your mother is dying of cancer or if you should file for divorce. Give yourself a chance to become comfortable with the process before venturing into areas that are emotionally loaded.

As you progress with your association with extraterrestrials, you'll notice that it's not so important to label them with a particular name or group. You'll discover that they too have little interest in being labeled or lumped into a particular name, category, or group. In the same way that you could spend an entire afternoon listing all the labels that partially describe you, the ETs may instead encourage you to get on with the dialogue that's important to your soul. Consider that we each have dozens of potential labels that only partially describe us. I'm a woman, an American, a mother, an author, a driver, a grocery shopper, a parent, a lover, a gardener, a traveler, etc. Do you see what I mean?

Enlightened beings bend, change, and shape-shift because they can. So how is it then that you expect them to remain unchanging and stay within the confines of just one label? They, like us, are multifaceted, multidimensional beings, living physical lives, but unlike us, they recognize their shape-shifting nature.

The Most Profound Question to Be Answered by ETs Is Not Who Are They, but Who Are You?

This is the essence of ET/human coaching. We're seeking to understand the true nature of *ourselves* so that we can get on with our evolution. This is precisely the type of inspiration that ETs provide. They encourage you to find your own truths, to know your own soul's agenda, to hear, finally, the voice of your own soul.

When you first make contact, if you feel a surge of joyous emotions, you've hit pay dirt. Your happy, emotional response is your omen, helping you to recognize that you remember something or someone whom you've forgotten about until now.

ET Reunions Are
Emotionally Potent

You may be surprised how emotional you feel once you make contact. If you become fearful, your intellect may simply be responding in a way that's consistent with our earthly culture of fear.

As far as the nature of ET communication is concerned, you will know the tree by its fruit. Gandhi, Buddha, and Jesus did not walk around instilling fear in the masses, nor did they encourage anyone to hurt or even judge another. Their message was one of non-judgment, peaceful surrendering to the now, recognizing one's spiritual nature, being inspired to feel safe in God's love and strength, and recognizing our true nature as powerful spiritual beings. If you receive a negative message, disconnect. You're not being sponsored by love.

Trust Yourself to Know
That You Can
Attract Goodness . . .
Trust Yourself to Know
How to Separate
from Another Whom
You Do Not Deem
to Embody Goodness

You may be wondering what to do if you connect to an undesirable visitor. When dealing with what you consider to be anyone or anything negative, just invite them to leave, and they usually will of their own accord. Show them the door and do not allow reentry. Once opened to contact, several beings may knock upon your door to gain entry, but you are in charge of the house, so do not let them in. You get to choose who to invite. You need not fear those who simply ask for an invitation. Eventually your energetic demeanor alone will attract a certain type of guest and the others will fall away.

It's like life in general: you're in charge of who you invite for dinner, who you marry or spend time with. You need not be a victim of anyone else's desire. When you know this in your heart, you will not reject out of hand a process of learning telepathy simply because you're concerned that you may meet someone undesirable. If you want to be open to love, you must be open to receiving love.

If you do connect with otherworldly beings and you feel fear, please refer to my lengthy discussion about fear in chapters 2, 3, and 4 in *Calling on Extraterrestrials*. Because of the culture that we grow up in, we have been conditioned to fear those who look dissimilar to us and who have different customs. So, just because you experience fear, it is not necessarily an indication that something bad is happening. If you have been taught through the cultural language and media to fear "evil aliens," then don't be surprised if you feel fear when you behold those whom you've been taught to fear. It takes moxie to be this kind of pioneer. If you don't have the emotional makeup to be a pioneer, find another adventure.

How Do You Know
You're Actually Talking
to Extraterrestrials?

At first, you may not. Telepathy is an introduction. Like all of your *other* relationships, it's up to you and the ETs to decide the quality and manner of your ongoing connection, if any. I'm suggesting that when you hear your first knock on the door, open it to see who's there. Become willing to meet others who may look and act differently but share our neighborhood and may want to get to know you too.

Telepathy allows you to explore the beginning stages of a new relationship. You are returning to a state where you remember your connection to ETs. Attempting the telepathic connection to extraterrestrials means that your soul has been stirred to try something. Why? Because many humans are deeply connected spiritually to extraterrestrials. Your soul knows what it's up to. Your curiosity and intrigue about ET contact is your "symptom" that your soul is ready to become a practicing member of the universe.

Do you think that your long-term fascination with all things UFO is a coincidence? There are no coincidences. There are no random experiences. Metamorphs are curious about the galaxy and those who live there. So if this describes you, and you also find yourself trying this process, it should give you pause. Telepathic coaching by extraterrestrials is getting your ET contacts under way.

Once you begin to communicate with ETs, establish the nature of your relationship together. Ask them to appear to you in a way and manner that best suits your soul's nature and purpose. Remember that they have come to assist you in your spiritual growth, so be open to listening to their suggestions. This is the importance of the pep talk part of your sessions. Being open to new ideas and then recording them is key to your progress. Keep track of your progress and record your experiences over the entire twelve-week process.

**Enlightened Beings
Do Not Give Orders
or Instruct Humans
on How to Live Their Lives.
They Make Suggestions.**

Coaches inspire us to find our own higher truths and to get in touch with our soul's agenda. You can ask them about the nature of your communication together, and even if you doubt what you hear, record it anyway. Are they here to assist you with your career or in finding your right livelihood? Will they help you in matters of love and intimacy, inspiring you to choose a partner that best resonates with your path? Perhaps your soul has volunteered to be the provider of technology or ideas that will transform the way humans presently do something. Whatever path you are on will determine the nature of their help.

What Else Can Happen?

- Soon after you begin practicing telepathy, you may begin to hear the thoughts of your friends or co-workers.
- You may begin to have dreams in which you are visited by extraterrestrials. Keep a record of all of your dreams and images.
- You may begin to hear the thoughts of animals or strongly sense what they want or need.
- You may be awakened by a dearly departed loved one, who returns to give you a message.
- You may be awakened by an explosion of light.

"Listen" with All Your Senses

When I was first contacted, I began to see colored bursts of light that would flash in front of me when someone spoke to me or when I was pondering some dilemma or question. Through trial and error, eventually I learned to decode the meaning behind each color and to this day, the lights inspire me to think differently, or to consider an option that I hadn't previously considered.

Once when I was out looking for houses to rent with a girlfriend, we thought that we had found the perfect house. As we discussed our options, my friend said, "I think this is the right house for us."

Immediately, there was a white strobe of light that appeared near her face. Since I had come to learn that, for me, the white light symbolized faulty or erroneous thinking or conclusions, I suggested that we keep looking. Sure enough, a week later we found a bigger and nicer house and rented it immediately.

Because I have become accustomed to identifying and then following this type of guidance and input from ETs, I manifested a more positive living situation for myself.

Another time, my assistant was in my office describing an idea she had for marketing one of our products. Immediately, a large aqua blue flash of light exploded near her. I knew that it was a sound idea and that we should proceed with it.

**Practice Receiving Guidance
with the Small Issues . . .
Then You'll Be Ready
to Get Help with the Big Ones**

The guidance you receive telepathically will build upon itself. You'll get help with minor or seemingly insignificant issues in order to build your confidence with larger issues.

For me, each year, the "stakes" get higher as I begin applying this help to bigger and bigger life strategies. In the early years I'd get trivial suggestions such as when I was in the grocery store picking out tomatoes and the ETs suggested which ones were sweet. These are practice sessions. Soon after, as I demonstrated my mastery in listening and acting upon trivial ideas and suggestions, more important issues surfaced. I've become confident with the telepathic input that I receive because I've been practicing on the little events that have made up my daily life. Now that I've gotten the hang of it, I confidently implement ET inspired strategies as they relate to the larger areas of my life. If I were to get a message to refrain from boarding an airplane as I'm checking in at the airport, I would confidently cancel my trip.

The Delayed Response Pep Talk Delivers Communion through Thought When You're Most Receptive

Sometimes your coach will deliver a pep talk after you end your session. You may be in the grocery store, car, shower, or in the middle of a horrible argument when you detect a word or phrase. It is very common for the pep talk to be delivered after you leave your chat room because at the time, you may not have been ready or capable of hearing it.

For this reason, don't judge your success by whether or not you receive a message while in your chat room. You may receive a life-altering message when you're standing at the curb taking the mail out of your mail box. This is called the Delayed Response Pep Talk and it happens all the time. Immediately write a note of what you hear or sense. You can ask about it during your next session. One student rarely received messages while in her chat room but she regularly began to hear coaching in the car. If this happens, don't stop your chat room practice sessions because they are probably responsible for preparing you for what you've received in your car. This should tell you that the process is working. Continue with your practice sessions until you are also able to receive messages in your chat room.

Head Buzzing Means
You're Connected to ETs

If you feel as though you've stuck your finger in a light socket, or if your head begins to vibrate, don't panic, you're just being zapped by universal energies from the higher realms. I've learned to pay attention to this if it happens when I'm about to make a decision, or if I'm following some line of thought or conversation.

Similar to colored flashes of light, head buzzing is like a gentle teacher tapping you on the shoulder and saying, "Excuse me, you may want to consider this other line of thinking (or acting) before you continue. You'll save yourself a whole lot of headaches later."

At such moments of input, I often excuse myself and go to a private, quiet place to center and "listen." Am I heading off-course? Am I thinking or acting in a way that is not consistent with my higher ideals? Is another person attempting to lead me astray or impose a faulty line of thinking on me?

Once you become adept at noticing that you're being tapped on the shoulder, it becomes your responsibility to glean what your next course of action might be. You may need to retreat to a quiet spot and mediate or go for a walk to be closer to God. The solution is always there waiting for us, if we only take a moment away from our rushed lives to listen.

The reason behind all of this input is that many of us are ready to take our lives to another level, and to begin practicing living more forthrightly according to higher principles. This is how we'll personally evolve. Our health will improve, our ability to manifest our dreams will be fine-tuned, and we will begin to function fully, abundantly, and joyously. A telepathic connection with enlightened beings helps sponsor us towards a life of thriving—not striving.

Each Moment Is Necessary
Along Our
Evolutionary Journey

Once you begin your journey with your extraterrestrial coaches, you will be charting a path that most of our species have never traveled—yet. Imagine the unique role that you're playing in the evolution of humanity as humans are introduced to the universe.

But it all starts with a telepathic introduction. Some of my former workshop students, and readers who have contacted me, were provided with an early draft of the manuscript. They provided me with comments and feedback that are included in this book. One student reports her initial telepathic sessions this way:

> The more I practice calling the ETs, the more I get used to what the feeling of their energy feels like. My first attempts were fun. The ETs really amuse me, which is not what I was expecting. I guess I was expecting a sort of stodgy race of beings, as though I had assumed that connecting with them would be like going to a class to get a lecture about being enlightened. They are fun and happy and light.
>
> Calling them and talking to them itself is fun. The goal of the communication would be to learn and experience but it is also fun in the process. It isn't like going to church. It's like hanging out with a group of great friends you never knew you had who also have great knowledge to share.

Several months after beginning these practice sessions, this student began to be visited by ETs while she slept and she reported to receive a lot of communication with them in her sleep. She began to sense a deepening of her relationship with them and her waking sessions continue to this day.

**Receiving Mentoring
from the Higher Realms
Will Constantly
Challenge You to
Be the Best You Can Be**

You will be constantly reminded to return to your "center" to feel empowered, not disempowered, and to trust that the answer to any problem or dilemma has a spiritual solution. When you establish ET contact, your connection is always with you wherever you go. Whether you are driving your car or sitting at your computer, once you become familiar with their "voice" you will be inspired and encouraged on a daily basis.

This is how, individually, we will become prepared to help our whole species become members of our universal community. When you are ready, your personal relationship and connection to ETs will assist you in expanding your ties with otherworldly beings in such a way that you will model to the world what is possible.

One Day Humans Will
Move About the Universe
More Freely, Having
Become Familiar with
Our Connection to
Our Wondrous
Universal Neighbors

Extraterrestrials have always been out there; they've only been awaiting our readiness to know them. Our spiritual heritage ensures that we're not restricted to experiencing just one realm. It's now time for us to embrace those other realms more purposefully. Establishing a relationship with extraterrestrials and being able to listen to their input will change your life in an extraordinary way.

To repeat, as you begin to use telepathy, you may not know for certain with whom you are talking. But once you are introduced, you can continue the communication and it will naturally develop into a broader relationship during which time you will know whom you've met.

Liken it to the Internet chat room that you're using for the first time. You log on, choose someone to chat with, and begin a conversation. The other person tells you a little about herself, and you share a bit about yourself. The first time you chat is just a start. At some point you may exchange names, then you may decide to meet face-to-face. What once began as an anonymous exchange in a chat room can grow into something intimate and personal. It all depends upon how you wish to proceed.

Learning telepathy allows you to begin this remarkable relationship.

Key Points:

- Self-doubt often sets in when we expand ourselves spiritually because the ego prefers to be dominant. Self-doubt is generated when the ego judges and criticizes our expanding spirituality.

- Recognize that you may be a metamorph, a pioneer whose soul blueprint is asking you to know extraterrestrials who can help and sponsor you.

- A telepathic connection is only an introduction. Stay with the process and much more can happen.

The Goal Is Not to Know
ETs Through and Through.
The Goal Is to Know Self
Through and Through.

Reminders:

1. Before you begin your first session, read through this book completely.
2. Sign your contract and tell the universe you're ready for contact.
3. Use the two pivotal tools of contact: the chatroom and the pep talk.
4. Establish your sacred chat room and prepare yourself and the room for contact.

   - Select and obtain a wonderful selection of music.
   - Set up two recorders: one for playing music and the other for recording your sessions.
   - Decorate your chat room with the "jewelry of the universe."
   - Light a candle or get a fire going in the fireplace to conjure up elemental energies.
   - Immerse yourself in water to open your chakras.

5. Begin your session.

   - Hook up your microphone and tape recorder.
   - Start the music and allow it to open the portal for you.
   - Allow yourself to fully relax and bring yourself to a state of bliss.
   - If you feel troubled or upset about your worldly problems or concerns, purge your troubles away by telling enlightened extraterrestrials about all that's troubling you.
   - Listen with all your senses and listen to your coach's pep talk.
   - Begin a two-way conversation and repeat out loud what you hear, even if it's one slow word at a time.
   - Ask the ETs questions out loud and repeat and record their responses.
   - Don't judge what you hear.

6. Record what you experience.

- What do you hear, see, feel, or sense?
- Do you feel head buzzing?
- Do you see flashes of light, images, or symbols?
- Understand the nature of self-doubt as it relates to this type of spiritual growth.
- Don't edit or censor yourself or the ETs. Trust in the process and have fun!
- Recognize the Delayed Response Pep Talk and allow for telepathy to reach you anytime, anywhere.

Final Thoughts

Many people on this planet have already had some sort of contact with extraterrestrial life, whether it's through vivid dreams, out-of-body experiences, seeing craft, or actual face-to-face encounters. The ETs themselves have told me that it is around 20 percent of the population, or over a *billion and a half* people. But many more haven't had these experiences, or for that matter even thought about it. Whether one has or hasn't, one may ask the question, "Why is it important?" In the final analysis, what does it matter, and why should we care? How will it affect our lives? Should we make an effort to contact these beings, and if so, what would we get out of it?

The answer to these questions will be personal to each of us. Some of you are simply curious about experiencing more of the universe. Others want specific help or guidance. No matter the reason for choosing to consciously invite ET contact, otherworldly beings await our readiness to know them. It is the process, the inner journey in which we become aware of our extraterrestrial neighbors that is so fascinating to me.

Nick is a sixteen-year-old Canadian teenager who read my first two books because he was intrigued with the idea of having ET contact. We began corresponding because he wanted desperately to be able to connect to ETs himself. After considering the ideas in my first two books, Nick wrote me, saying that he had actually begun to have "zapping" experiences at night and had begun to see flashes of light out of the corner of his eye. I encouraged him to keep going with his process of inwardly and consciously inviting contact.

Then after a few months, he thought he may have actually had an encounter experience, although he wondered if perhaps it was a lucid dream. He was thrilled. He described an ET who appeared in front of him, and started to move closer to him. A conversation ensued, although he can't remember it exactly. But generally, he remembered asking the ET, "Can I meet one of your people face to face in the physical?"

"It will take time," the ET replied.

"But I really want to meet soon," Nick said.

"We are very popular, so it'll take time," the ET said.

Was Nick's experience a dream? Was it his wishful thinking? Did he accurately remember the communication? Whatever happened, the experience propelled Nick to want to know more. He's been diligently practicing the techniques outlined in this book ever since, motivated, he says by the yearning to "have the best teachers to show me the way to live life." Nick explains:

> To be able to establish contact with ETs would have to be one of the most awesome fantasy experiences come true for me. To just find out about their lives would be enough on one level. It would prove to me personally that we are not alone in the universe. This in itself would be a life-altering spiritual experience. To be mentored, to have paranormal experiences open up, and telepathy with animals and people

as a result of the ETs would be wonderful. To have physical and mental enhancements and better health as a result of contact or their technology would be frosting on the cake and reinforce how wonderful the universe is and that fantasy really can become reality. To be happy, joyful, thriving, and living my dreams of helping the world being the grandest version of the greatest vision I can behold as part of the contact, I see nothing but positive love coming from all this. Of course challenges come with this new opening, awakening, etc., as well.

A few weeks after Nick tried the techniques in this book, he contacted me again. He was frustrated. "I'm sorry to bother you, but I need your help with this. I've been trying these techniques for three weeks, every day for one hour, but I haven't had anything else happen. Can you give me some more tips? Sometimes I really feel like I'm just talking to the ceiling. How do the ETs know that I'm trying to talk to them?"

I explained to Nick that as spiritual, evolved beings, ETs understand that all information is available, everywhere. In other words, the universe is an open book, if we know that it is. So as evolved beings, they tap into this universal knowing and are open to hearing, receiving, and providing help in the same manner that we imagine other spiritual guides are always available to us for help. As for being able to detect telepathy consciously, I agree that the very first time can be difficult. This is what I told Nick:

This is one of the hardest parts about learning this language: to be able to detect telepathy the very first time. Also, telepathy can be accompanied by images, symbols, tones, feelings, and knowing. They inspire us through our imagination. I do understand your frustration. But stay with it, because you're very close to breaking through.

Next session, as you're relaxing and listening, imagine

that you're listening with the top part of your body, instead of just your ears. So let go of the idea that your ears will hear words in the way that you're accustomed to hearing words. Pretend that your body is a big piece of clay, and the first word or few words that you "hear" will actually be "pressed" ever so gently into your clay body. There may be a very, very slight pressure, or presence of a word that wants to form in your thoughts, while simultaneously being gently "pressed" into your clay being. Or, instead of a word or phrase, you may receive a visual image that may appear to you in the dark to help you hear the word.

For example, once a friend of mine named Bev had phoned to tell me how upset she was that she had misplaced her airline tickets. They were not e-tickets, but hard copies of tickets that are just like cash. She had been saving for a long time to take a trip to Europe and her tickets represented several thousand dollars worth of air travel. They could not be replaced if lost or stolen.

Knowing that a telepathic connection to ETs is readily available to me, I wanted to help her. Immediately, I closed my eyes, centered myself, and asked the ETs if they could help. Instantly, I saw an image of a hand. I did not hear any words.

"Bev, I'm seeing an image of a hand, or maybe it's a glove. Are the tickets next to your gloves, or in the glove compartment of your car?" I asked her. Bev trotted off to look for the tickets on her closet shelf where her gloves were kept. Next she checked the glove compartment of her car. "No, they're not there," she said disappointedly. "I guess they're just lost. Now what am I going to do?"

"Well, wait a minute. Help me brainstorm this. I'm not hearing any words, yet, so let's just go with the image." Again, I got another strong visual image of a pair of hands, but I could detect no words. "Bev, where are you at this very moment, as you're talking to me on the phone?" I asked her.

"Sitting at my desk," she said, sounding more and more dejected.

At that moment, I also heard two words.

"Bev, I got it. I just heard the words 'at hand.' Your tickets are at hand. They must be right near you, right there on your desk, but perhaps they're tucked inside an envelope or something. They're right there at hand."

The receiver of the phone clunked on the desk as Bev must have dropped the phone. I could hear her madly shuffling through papers. Several minutes passed, with Bev's voice giving me a blow by blow. "Let's see, here's the gas bill that I need to pay. Oh, here's that receipt I couldn't find. . . . Oh my god, here they are! The tickets. They were right here 'at hand' in this huge pile the whole time."

In this example with Bev's missing airline tickets, I just allowed myself to go with the guidance. Sometimes it can be an image, a word, or an impression that comes through before any telepathic words. Whatever it is that you receive, go with it. Let it pick you up and take you away. You're entering a stream of consciousness, that once detected, will serve you your whole life.

Another time, a different friend phoned me very upset about the breakup of her relationship. As I struggled for the right words to comfort her, an image appeared to me of a baby pacifier. I had no clue what it meant, or how it related to my friend's grief. But instead of allowing myself to become frustrated, I stayed with it and asked for more clarification. Prior to detecting any telepathic words, I kept seeing the image of a baby pacifier. I wondered what on earth this image had to do with my friend or her predicament. Several minutes later, I heard two words: "Pacify her." The image was used as a pun to help me connect to the idea behind the forthcoming words. I was being encouraged to "bring or restore her to a state of peace or tranquility" by offering her my time, and words of encouragement.

Do you see how this language works? Telepathy "arrives" in many ways. You never know if your communication will arrive as a phone call, an e-mail, a head buzz, a knowing, telepathic words—or all of the above. Enlightened beings use all manner of contrivances to communicate and to help you to learn and detect their presence.

No matter how silly it feels, or no matter how certain you are that you're making it up or imagining this new voice or impression, simply try it again. Listen for one word, or two words, or look for an image, no matter how faint. Repeat the word out loud or describe the image out loud, even if you think that you're not really hearing it or detecting it. Repeat it out loud as though you are translating this new voice for someone else's benefit. Of course, this is so you can capture the words on your tape recorder.

Next, *respond* to the voice—the word, or question, or sentence—*even if you're 99 percent certain it's just your wishful thinking or overactive imagination*. You will ask yourself to suspend your disbelief, and simply play a wonderful game for an hour, if this is the way to create an atmosphere of limitlessness.

For example, suppose you think you feel the word "hello" pressed into your clay body. But you're not sure. Go with it anyway, despite your doubts. Don't censor. Remember, this is a training. You're practicing. No one need know what you are doing or why. Pretend that the "hello" that you felt and "heard" was real, and continue. What is the next word you hear and feel? If you feel self-conscious, knowing that your tape recorder is burning tape with nothing happening, just turn it off for the session.

You're playing now, dancing with the energies from on

high. Do you feel it? If I offered you a million dollars right at that moment to tell me what word you're hearing, what would the word or phrase be? Imagine that the voice doesn't get "louder" until you recognize it, then once you do, it will be plenty loud enough because you'll sense its origin and its nature and you'll know it as the telepathy that it is.

You may feel silly as you try this. The voice of your mind's protest may sound much louder than anything else. That's okay. This is a natural part of the transition. Stay with it. Try to hear just one word, or two words, or a few words and repeat them out loud and respond. And keep going. If you want to kick it up a notch, set the alarm and try this between the wee hours of 1:00 A.M. and 4:00 A.M. You may find the voice to be more potent then.

Michael, an ordained minister, contacted me after reading my first two books. He himself has had many ET encounters and was interested in receiving a copy of this book so that he could practice the techniques I suggested to develop more conscious contact and to learn to initiate the contact at will. Like Michael, there are millions of people worldwide who have already established a relationship with ETs but they're looking to continue the relationship in a more conscious way. Michael has just started practicing the sessions and I'm eager to know if this book helps him to develop more of a sense of controlling the direction of his contacts at will. Michael explains:

> Usually I wait until I hear from the ETs as part of physical visits at night or through telepathy when I am meditating. Perhaps my motivation is my need for more control, but this is my desire. After my visitations I am usually much more physically and emotionally calm and centered. This usually occurs a day or so afterwards. At times I am extremely tired after a visit. The best way I can explain it is that there is "a

219

peace beyond all understanding." It appears that afterwards I am much more centered and that I can face the joys as well as the slings and arrows of outrageous fortune that life sometimes brings. I currently reside in New York City. Need I say more?

Kathleen is a massage therapist and healer from New Hampshire who contacted me regarding her own ongoing ET contacts. She's had regressions with a UFO investigator in trying to glean more conscious memory as to the nature and content of her contacts. She was thrilled at the possibility of using the techniques in this book as an adjunct to her process. Regarding her motivation to continue ET contact, Kathleen wrote to me:

> Dear Lisette, I truly want ongoing contact to learn. We are destroying our planet at a rapid rate and whatever we can learn from others who have been there before is crucial at this point. I am a healer and feel there must be more I can learn in the use of energy that would affect my life and the lives of others.
>
> I can't thank you enough for this material. I couldn't read through it fast enough. I was so absorbed in it and had the feeling of immense joy. I thought it would take a few weeks to get results but in less than one week, I'm already getting results! I've begun to be awakened to a telepathic voice, and am now using two recorders. Really good suggestion! Thanks to your suggestion in using two tape recorders, I've been able to record the message for replay the next morning. I've been asking the ETs specific questions about protection and how to heal my shoulder and have received an answer. Ever since I started this book, things have been transpiring at a rapid rate. Ask and you shall receive—almost instantly.

Doug is a 52-year-old high school science teacher in the Midwest who contacted me about his own ongoing ET contact. He describes his reaction in reading this material for the first time:

> I got goosebumps reading what you had written, exclaiming out loud to an empty house, perhaps with invisible shape-shifted ETs nearby, "That's exactly what happened to me!" or "Oh my God, how could she know this?"

Doug is working on his own book, and is also consciously being assisted by enlightened beings. He explains:

> Lisette, in the 52 years that I have been involved with my own encounter phenomena, your books have given me more goosebumps of recognition and delight than anything I have ever read in my entire life.
>
> My intent in contacting ETs is manifold. It would reaffirm my long-held belief that we are not alone in this vast universe. Having friends and traveling companions among the star lanes of just the Milky Way alone makes the thought of deep space a much more palatable one. Since they have come to visit us, that suggests to me that they are more advanced in many ways than we are. There must be all kinds of cultural and cosmic protocols of which we are completely unaware, but which we could learn from them and their galactic neighbors. As a teacher, I value the chances to learn new things and explore new worlds, whether they are under the lens of a microscope, at the other end of my computer keyboard, or stretched out across this arm of the Milky Way.
>
> The effect that ET contact has had on me already allows me to encompass new belief systems and free myself of some of the cumbersome ones we have here on Earth. Contact with ETs opens the mind. For me, this is just a beginning. I have discovered heretofore-unknown capabilities that I am beginning to exercise for the first time. These include healing, precognitive dreaming, weather control, and random materialization of small objects.

Many people have asked me the significance of decorating their chat rooms with stones, rocks, or flowers, etc. Aku, an intitiated elder and shaman by birth and training lives in West Africa. She contacted me, explaining that she has had ongoing ET contact, but also through the stones:

> I work very closely with the stone spirits and have done so for thirteen years now. There are many stones that are linked directly to Star People and they have been close companions of mine for some time. The stones actually share beautiful words and understanding from the other worlds and like the relationship with the Star People, I treasure how we all engage together.

Whether we connect to spirit guides, angels, animal totems, extraterrestrials, or even stones, the universe is always awaiting our readiness to peel back another layer of the onion in which we will know more. Our motivations are many, but the possibilities are limitless.

During this twelve-week process, you may feel that nothing at all has happened. If this occurs, please do not give up. Often, there is a delayed response, and you will make your first telepathic connection at the gas station or while you're stuck in gridlock. A delayed reaction to your efforts may pleasantly surprise you, just when you thought no progress was being made. Know that if you are called to this material, then you will be successful in retrieving your connection to extraterrestrials. If you get discouraged, please read the following, even if you have to read it every single day:

> "When nothing seems to help, I go and look at a stonecutter, hammering away at his rock perhaps a hundred times without as much as a crack showing in it. Yet at the hundred and first blow it will split in two, and I know it was not that blow that did it, but all that had gone before together."
> —Jacob Riis, author of *The Making of an American*
> (New York: Macmillan, 1903)

Don't give up. The fulfillment of your dreams may require you to be coached and your soul may have set it up that ETs are your best sponsor. So don't give up on your dreams. Stay connected to others who are seeking to bring their life to a new level.

You have come here to do something special. You have a special gift to offer the world that only you can provide in your unique way. Your individual fingerprint makes your special gift, and the way and manner that you offer it, uniquely original. Your ET coach and all of the universe are counting on you to move to self-mastery and effectuate something wondrous.

I'm counting on you to e-mail me or write me a letter and let me know how you're progressing so that I may include some of your anonymous stories of inspiration and hope in upcoming books. I also offer an on-line course using a guided meditation. Refer to my website at www.talkingtoETs.com.

Meeting extraterrestrials is the greatest story of all time. And you do not have to be alone in pursuing this worthiest of endeavors. As of this writing, spontaneous groups are already forming and my former students have already reported amazing and encouraging results. These students are going on to lead their own groups. In this way, exciting information is coming through, both for personal fulfillment and also for group and planetary healing.

Blessings on your continued adventure,

—Lisette Larkins

Lisette can be contacted
by e-mail at:

Lisette@talkingtoETs.com

or by writing to her at:

Lisette Larkins
c/o Hampton Roads Publishing Co.
1125 Stoney Ridge Road
Charlottesville, VA 22902

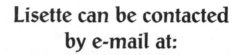

Epilogue

". . . but Mom," the young one asked his mother, "how do I know they'll
be able to hear me when I use telepathy?"

"Because dear, all information is available to everyone, everywhere.
Besides," his mother responded with a twinkle in her eye, "I happen
to know first-hand that relationships between our species can be
initiated solely by our willingness."

"Mom, you mean you've actually met them?" the child asked excitedly.

The woman smiled and her eyes began to tear.
She looked out her window
at the sun that was setting on the mountains in the distance,
remembering her very first contact so long ago.
"Yes, not only have we been introduced but
we remain close to this day and speak often."

"But Mom, why did they choose you?"

"They didn't, dear. We chose each other as friends.
It was our mutual soul plans."

"I want that to be part of my soul plan too," the child said emphatically.

The mother sees a burst of blue light erupt near the child's face,
recognizing it as a sign that she's speaking a higher truth and that
her child's desire is a higher truth, too.

"When you decide something and choose to make it part of your
dreams and your hopes, the universe conspires to help it come true.
Magically, your dreams become your soul plan and part of your destiny."

The child smiled broadly at his mother, and his mother felt that her
heart would burst.
She took her son's small hand in her own, and together
they walked out the door to enjoy the sunset together.

About the Author

Lisette Larkins speaks internationally in the field of UFO phenomena and extraterrestrial communication. She has appeared on hundreds of radio programs, and her books are in the process of being developed into a feature film. You can find additional information about her appearances and on-line course by visiting her web site:

www.talkingtoETs.com

Hampton Roads Publishing Company
. . . for the evolving human spirit

Hampton Roads Publishing Company
publishes books on a variety of subjects including
metaphysics, health, visionary fiction, and other related topics.

For a copy of our latest catalog,
call toll-free, 800-766-8009,
or send your name and address to:

Hampton Roads Publishing Company, Inc.
1125 Stoney Ridge Road
Charlottesville, VA 22902
e-mail: hrpc@hrpub.com
www.hrpub.com